Market and Sales Forecasting

Market and Sales Forecasting

A QUANTITATIVE APPROACH

Norbert Lloyd Enrick

Kent State University

CHANDLER PUBLISHING COMPANY

124 Spear Street, San Francisco, California 94105

Science Research Associates, Inc., 259 East Erie Street, Chicago, Illinois 60611
Distributors   A Subsidiary of IBM

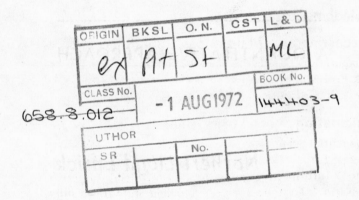

658.818
ENR

Contents

Tables

Figures

Foreword

Efficiency, profitability, and long-term survival in today's highly competitive marketplace is a matter of concern to multitudes of business firms. New products, new services, and other innovations are streaming in at ever increasing rates; at the same time, the pace of technological development and product obsolescence is also accelerating. Concomitantly, marketing costs are rising not only in terms of promotion but also in terms of personnel skills and the quality of services required.

While the demands for executive skills, experience, and judgment must inevitably rise, in order to meet the challenges of good management, it is also abundantly clear that quantitative tools of analysis are needed as aids. Current factors, situations, and developments require analytical treatment for weighing portents and developing forecasts. Executives, working with analysts, not only will assure better quantitative methods, but also will be able to sharpen their own judgments and enhance the quality of their decisions.

It is not for sales and marketing alone that forecasts are needed. Long before the first sale is made, production and inventories must be planned. Moreover, if a firm is to keep pace with the need for innovation, then the research and development work required calls for intense efforts months and years before production is even contemplated. Throughout, thought must be given to the systems aspects of management. Sales, marketing, inventories, production, and product innovation are parts of an integrated network that must be organized, planned, nurtured, and constantly improved if the firm is to survive and grow. Proper planning, to assure efficient and profitable operation of the system as a whole, calls for carefully weighed and soundly arrived at forecasts of markets expected and sales volume considered achievable.

The purpose of this book is to provide forecasting methods and procedures for both the short range and the long range. Only the principal techniques which have been found practical and useful in the experience of the past two decades are provided. These techniques are heavily oriented in the direction of (1) quantitative methods and (2) the systems approach of management. Every effort has been made to present the quantitative procedures in a clear, ready-to-use manner. Support for the methods recommended is given in terms of practical explanations and an appeal to intuitive understanding, since it is believed that the busy manager and executive need not be concerned with the more rigorous though "impeccable" mathematical derivations that may be found elsewhere.

The author's claim for competence in preparing this practice-oriented book is experience, in the course of two decades, in consulting work for managements of nearly fifty organizations—small, medium, and gigantic. Most of the material in this book has been previously used in executive, managerial, and industrial short courses. The comments, criticism, and helpful discussion by many of the thousands of people who have attended these courses—as well as my experience in teaching regular college-level courses in the subject—have been of value to me in writing a book that, hopefully, will facilitate the use of modern methods and techniques for forecasting.

NORBERT LLOYD ENRICK

Kent, Ohio

Acknowledgments

Experience in actual applications, supported by study and development research, form the basis of this book. For the opportunity to participate in market- and sales-forecasting programs and to evaluate the relative merit, effectiveness, and validity of a variety of techniques, I am indebted to the large number of business organizations for whom I have performed consulting work during the past decade.

The ultimate form in which this material is being presented has evolved slowly, as a result of college courses and special programs for managers, executives, and staff people. I am indebted to these groups for their comments, criticisms, and other valuable contributions.

Finally, before going into book form, many of the key chapters were published in the pages of *Industrial Canada,* a journal of the Canadian Manufacturers' Association. A. W. House, editor of the journal, made numerous revisions and related improvements in each article as it appeared in that journal, and all of these contributions have been maintained in the present text.

Leonard J. Konopa and Jim L. Grimm, Professors of Marketing, and Donald F. Mulvihill, Chairman of the Marketing Department at Kent State University, were kind enough to review various sections of the manuscript and made many helpful suggestions.

Market and Sales Forecasting

CHAPTER **1**

Forecasting as a Management Planning Aid

The prime purpose of this book is to develop an arsenal of practical forecasting methods, useful in marketing, sales, and other areas of management operations. We will examine the principal forecasting techniques and explore the ways in which they work. Methods for dealing with such factors as risk and uncertainty will be given attention. Procedures will be given for assessing the likely ranges of error associated with specific forecasts and for determining the degree of confidence which can be placed in these predictions. The scientific approach incorporated in such systems will give results that should be far more reliable and useful for management planning than mere guesstimates, opinions, or unstructured judgments. Support of evaluations and forecasts in terms of quantitative data will be stressed as part of the scientific method of modern management.

Reliable forecasting rests on a number of crucial principles which will be explored in this chapter. First and foremost is the need for close collaboration between management and analyst in developing forecasts. There must also be a feedback process that serves to revise forecasts on a timely basis, utilizing the current developmental trends in sales, markets, and other areas of concern. Data flows must be smooth, providing essential data with minimal delay. Finally, a systems approach should be utilized, so that as much of the work as possible can be done routinely.

COLLABORATION BETWEEN MANAGEMENT AND ANALYST

Today's executive is well aware of the need for understanding methodologies in depth. If he knows only the vocabulary and has only vague notions of actual methodology, he will be unable to achieve a high degree of collaboration with the forecasting analyst in arriving at

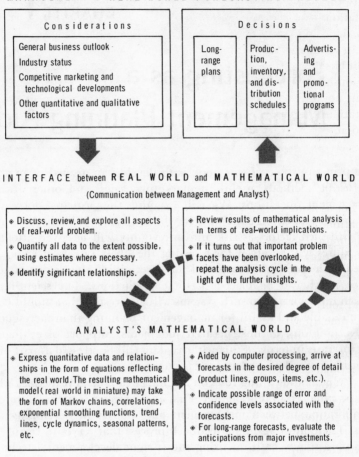

FIGURE 1–1. *Collaboration between management and analyst.*

really meaningful results. The essentials of this requirement for integrated effort will be stressed at various points throughout this book. They are brought out formally by the flow diagram of information, analysis, and decision processes in Figure 1–1. The interface, or middle section, of this figure shows how the interplay of information and ideas between the mathematically versed analyst and the managing executive is used advantageously. Unless the manager is aware of the major functions of the analytical tools to be used—their raw-data requirements, their basic procedures, the types of results obtainable, and their limitations—he is unlikely to supply the analyst with all pertinent facts, data, and relationships.

In turn, the analyst must have sufficient understanding of real-world business problems to grasp their significant meanings and inter-relationships. The choice of analytical tool will depend to a large extent not only on the purposes of the forecast but also on the factual limitations that apply to various alternative decisions at management's disposal.

FEEDBACK PROCESS

Let us assume that the analyst has received the pertinent data, information on significant relationships, and other materials needed for mathematical analysis. He will then express these real-world items in mathematical equations of relationship. The latter are often termed "the model," because they mirror in mathematical miniature the actual forecasting problem of real-world factors. Using appropriate analytical tools and with the aid of computer processing, the analyst will then come up with relevant forecasts and related information.

Next, the analyst will discuss the outcomes with the executive and other management people concerned. For one thing, the data derived by the analyst need interpretation in terms of their real-world decision-making implications. For another—and often more importantly so—it will usually develop from the outcomes of the forecast that certain facets do not agree with all of the anticipations derived from managerial evaluation and judgment. It is then said that there are "many unexpected results," and the following procedure seems indicated:

1. Review the original data and assumptions. Make such revisions as may be needed, and then rerun the analysis.

2. If no revisions are found necessary as a result of reviewing the original data and assumptions, devise some supplementary analyses. These analyses, using additional data and relationships, will then either confirm or modify the original forecasts.

3. Discuss the findings from the new analysis (step 1 or step 2 or both). If the new look at the problem has yielded no significant new aspects, then the original forecast may have been right after all. On the other hand, a modified result may be obtained that will now agree better with purely qualitative managerial anticipations.

This feedback loop of analysis and review may continue through several cycles until management is satisfied. In any event, it is up to management to make the final decisions on long-range planning; schedules for production, inventories, and distribution; and programs for advertising and other promotional endeavors.

While it is quite common to have to go through the feedback loop at least once or twice, it is rather unlikely that there will be any large *ultimate* discrepancies between managerial qualitative expectation and quantitative forecasts. The latter serve primarily as a confirmation of anticipations, with the added advantage of precise expectation data broken down in such detail as desired (products, time periods, market areas, and the like).

SMOOTH DATA FLOW

A look at the feedback mechanism is provided by Figure 1–2, which emphasizes data flows and the details of coming up with specific predictions for various products and successful future time periods. A further breakdown by market and distribution areas is also possible. While Figure 1–1 emphasized the general aspects of integrated efforts by management and analyst, Figure 1–2 examines the details of individual data as used in coming up with forecasts.

A SYSTEMS APPROACH

Executives should not be unduly burdened by the analysis process or by the need to assist the analyst in grasping the essential aspects and crucial interactions of the real-world problem. Once a good framework of forecasting has been worked out and tested in actual practice, routines can be established. Systems and procedures will then take over as automatic executors of management's aims and intentions.

The function of systems is clear. A system relieves executives, management, and staff personnel of tedious routines or repetitive tasks. The people concerned are thus freed to take on other responsibilities within the organization. Care must be taken, however, to incorporate within a system such automatic signaling devices (control limits, for example, as will be discussed) that bring management, executives, and staff prominently back into the evaluation process when a change in the underlying factors so demands.

In any event, the system is not a "set it, then forget it" device.

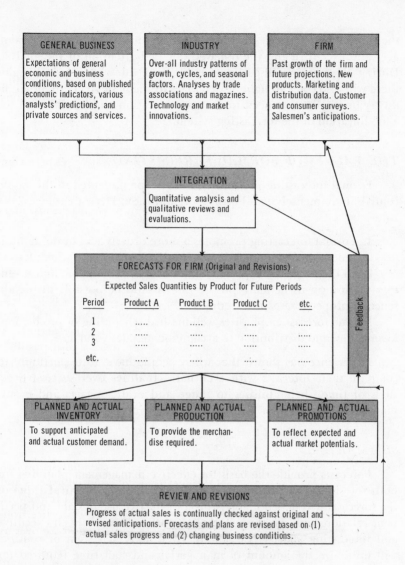

FIGURE 1–2. *Forecasting and planning in a firm.*

With the progress of time, as the frameworks supporting old forecasts are superseded, new predictions and predictive systems will be required. This statement applies to problems of season-to-season anticipations as well as to long-range planning. All these are occasions when

Forecasting as a Planning Aid 5

the procedures in Figures 1–1 and 1–2 demand the return of the manager and executive and the renewed detailed attention of the analyst. During the ensuing discussions, work, and interchange of thought, there will also come to light any changes in the basic structure of an industry or market that need further consideration and possibly call for a modification of the forecasting system.

THE VALUES OF FORMAL FORECASTING

Formal forecasting procedures, of the type presented in this book, contribute immensely to a business organization. Here are some of the values:

1. Formal forecasting promotes a more orderly way of doing business in general, based on definite expectations, plans, and schedules.

2. In the long run, expected data for sales, production, and inventory planning will be more precise than would be possible in the absence of proper forecasting methods.

3. The forecast emphasizes well-meshed scheduling of production, inventories, and distribution to accommodate sales volume.

Experience has shown that when people have an opportunity to compare their forecasts with eventual actualities over successive periods of time, their abilities to judge and evaluate facts and events sharpen—and thus their forecasting abilities improve.

SUMMARY

Forecasts provide the basis for effective management planning for both the short and the long run. The validity and practical value of the forecasts will depend largely on the effective use of data and pertinent relationships. To this end, collaborative effort between executive and forecasting analyst is essential. Eventually, a system of routines will minimize the amount of managerial and staff time required for forecasting and planning details.

CHAPTER 2

Anticipating Short-Term Demand

Customer service in an economical and effective manner calls for the anticipation of demand for merchandise, so that orders can be filled without undue delays because of stockouts. Such service, in turn, means that we must translate anticipated demand into proper planning for production, keeping in mind production rates within the organization and lead times for supplies, parts, and components purchased from outside suppliers.

When a large number and variety of items are sold, it becomes impossible to make individual forecasts of anticipated demand on the basis of personal judgment. We need a system that works automatically, monitors itself on a continuous basis, and trips a signal calling for management's attention only in instances where there is real need. The inventory must be balanced to obtain a reasonable degree of service efficiency consistent with the cost of inventory investment.

Attainment of balanced inventories thus hinges on a forecasting procedure that properly anticipates demand from period to period. The length of the period, usually, is the replenishment lead time. This span includes the interval from the moment that stocks have reached a low enough point to warrant issuance of a replenishment order (either from one's own plant-production facilities or from suppliers) to the normally expected time at which the new stock will have been added to inventory.

EXPONENTIAL SMOOTHING

For the purpose of forecasting demand from period to period, a technique known as *exponential smoothing* has achieved widespread popularity in industry, so that most manufacturers of computer hardware now have ready-made programs for such applications. It must be emphasized, however, that despite the availability of such "canned" programs, the installation and use of exponential smoothing for demand forecasting is still dependent on the ability of individual managements to adapt the system to the particular needs of an organization.

While the illustrative example in the following section is "shrunk to size" for paper-and-pencil application, it should nevertheless be adequate to convey the essential principles that the executive must understand in conjunction with the installation and operation of exponential smoothing in his organization.

ILLUSTRATIVE EXAMPLE

The nature of exponential smoothing is perhaps best demonstrated by an illustrative example. Let us assume 10 time periods, as in column *a* of Table 2–1. Each period may represent 4 weeks, or some other interval corresponding to the lead-time allowances discussed above. Actual demand during these periods, in units of the particular product involved, is shown in column *b*. Let us now assume that period 1 has just been completed, with an actual sales demand of 80 units. We are faced with the need to forecast demand for the next period. Certainly, the current demand has some bearing on the future. Also of significance is the earlier forecast. In particular, for the period immediately preceding the one just completed, a demand of 70 had been forecast.

To predict expected demand in period 2, how much importance or weight should be given the old forecast as against the actual sales in period 1? The answer to this question will be discussed later. For the moment, assume that we give a weight of 20 per cent to current actual sales. Then, the remaining 80 per cent of weight must go to the old forecast, to make up a total of 100 per cent. Expressed as a decimal fraction, 20 per cent becomes 0.2, which is known as the *smoothing factor* or *smoothing constant,* often denoted by the Greek letter alpha α. Next, $1 - \alpha = \beta$, the Greek letter beta for the weight assigned to the old forecast. At the end of period 1, we obtain a forecast of 72 units for period 2 from the following calculations:

$$\alpha \times \text{(Actual Demand)} + \beta \times \text{(Old Forecast)} = \text{New Forecast}$$
$$0.2 \times 80 + 0.8 \times 70 = 72$$

Next, noting that in period 2 actual demand was 90, we forecast

TABLE 2–1. PERIOD-TO-PERIOD DEMAND FORECAST BASED ON EXPONENTIAL
SMOOTHING, WITH A SMOOTHING FACTOR OF 0.2

a	b	c	d	e	f
Time Period	Actual Demand, in Units	Weighted Actual Demand, b × 0.2, in Units	Weighted Old Forecast,* e × 0.8, in Units	New Forecast,† c + d, in Units	Amount by Which Forecast Is High (+) or Low (−), e of Prior Row Minus b of Current Row, in Units
prior	—	—	—	(70)	—
1	80	16	56	72	−10
2	90	18	58	76	−18
3	110	22	61	83	−34
4	95	19	66	85	−12
5	105	21	68	89	−20
6	120	24	71	95	−31
7	105	21	76	97	−10
8	130	26	78	104	−33
9	125	25	83	108	−21
10	135	27	86	113	−27
Total	1,095	219	703	922	216
Average	110	22	70	92	22‡

* The old forecast is taken from the immediately prior period. Thus, for period 1, the prior forecast is 70, and 70 × 0.8 gives 56. For period 2, 72 × 0.8 gives 58. Data were rounded for simplicity.

† In each row, the new forecast is that which is made currently for the immediately following period. Thus, in period 1, we made a forecast of 72 units for period 2. Next, in period 2, actual demand turns out to be 90. The difference, $72 - 90 = -18$, shown in column f, represents the forecast error.

‡ In totaling column f, ignore minus signs (consider them as plus signs). The total of the 10 values is 215, which averages to $215/10 = 21.5$, or 22 rounded as the Mean Absolute Deviation (MAD). The term *absolute* refers to the fact that minus signs were ignored in the addition.

at the end of the period the new sales expectation as 76, since:

$$0.2 \times 90 + 0.8 \times 72 = 76$$

These calculations are revealed in columns c, d, and e of Table 2–1. The final column, f, shows the forecast error. Thus, we had predicted a demand of 70 units in period 1, but 80 were actually called for, so that the forecast was 10 units low. Our new forecast of 72 is again short, this time by 18 units, against the actual demand of 90 in period 2.

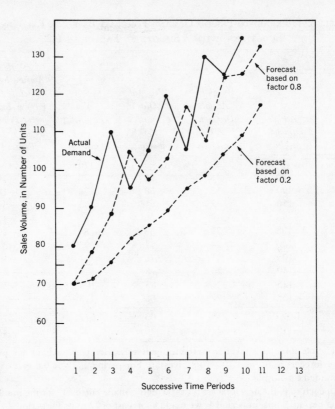

FIGURE 2–1. *Actual demand compared with forecasts.* The forecasts based on a smoothing factor of 0.8 come much closer to actuality than do the forecasts based on 0.2. Nevertheless, the fact that even the better forecast tends to lag somewhat behind actual demand suggests that a more refined forecasting method, such as *double smoothing,* may be needed.

MEASURING FORECAST ERROR

Examination of the tabulated results, supplemented by the graph in Figure 2–1, reveals that our forecasts are relatively poor. The forecast of sales demand is lagging behind the actual fast-rising trend. For the purpose of measuring forecasting error, it is not enough, however, to call a forecast "good," "poor," or some other qualitative designation. Instead, we need a measurable, comparable value such as that provided by the *mean absolute deviation* (MAD), to be discussed next.

a	b	c	d	e	f
Time Period	Actual Demand, in Units	Weighted Actual Demand, $b \times 0.4$, in Units	Weighted Old Forecast, $e \times 0.6$, in Units	New Forecast, $c + d$, in Units	Amount by Which Forecast Is High $(+)$ or Low $(-)$, e of Prior Row Minus b of Current Row, in Units
prior	—	—	—	(70)	—
1	80	32	42	74	−10
2	90	36	44	80	−16
3	110	44	48	92	−30
4	95	38	55	93	−3
5	105	42	56	98	−12
6	120	48	59	107	−22
7	105	42	64	106	+2
8	130	52	64	116	−24
9	125	50	70	120	−9
10	135	54	72	126	−15
Total	1,095	438	574	1,012	143
Average	110	44	57	101	14*

* Mean absolute deviation (MAD).

Let us look at the individual forecast errors in column *f* of Table
2–1. They all happen to be negative, but, for some other series, they
could easily have been positive, or some positive and others negative.
For the purpose of the mean absolute deviation, we are not interested
in whether an error is of the plus or minus (high or low) type, but
rather in its absolute magnitude. By "absolute" we mean that we wish
to consider each value regardless of sign. In adding absolute values, we
look on them as *all* positive (even if there is a minus sign in the column). The total of all 10 entries in *f*, taken as positive, is 216, giving
an average of 22 (rounded for simplicity). This average, or "mean," of
the absolute deviations of the forecast from the actual values is the
mean absolute deviation (MAD).

The smaller the MAD, the better is our forecasting method. For
example, we might ask: Would a smoothing factor of 0.4 have given us
a better forecast? Table 2–2 shows this approach, with a value of 14 for
MAD. Since this figure is less than the preceding 22, we conclude that a
factor of 0.4 is indeed preferable by giving a more accurate forecast.
Smoothing factors of 0.6 and 0.8 are also studied, with resultant fur-

a	b	c	d	e	f
Time Period	Actual Demand, in Units	Weighted Actual Demand. $b \times 0.6$, in Units	Weighted Old Forecast, $e \times 0.4$, in Units	New Forecast, $c + d$, in Units	Amount by Which Forecast Is High $(+)$ or Low $(-)$, e of Prior Row Minus b of Current Row, in Units
prior	—	—	—	(70)	—
1	80	48	28	76	−10
2	90	54	30	84	−14
3	110	66	34	100	−26
4	95	57	40	97	+5
5	105	63	39	102	−8
6	120	72	41	113	−18
7	105	63	45	108	+8
8	130	78	43	121	−22
9	125	75	48	123	−4
10	135	81	49	130	−12
Total	1,095	657	397	1,054	127
Average	110	66	40	105	13*

* Mean absolute deviation (MAD).

ther improvements of forecasting accuracy, as revealed in Tables 2–3 and 2–4 for 13 and 12 units of MAD.

Graphing the results, we note that we have come close to a minimal value. It is true that slightly higher values of the smoothing factor will give still smaller MAD's, but we cannot have a factor greater than 1.0, and we are close to that limit. Therefore, not much further improvement can be expected. The leveling off of the curve of MAD's in Figure 2–2 (p. 14) underscores this fact.

DETERMINING THE MOST SUITABLE SMOOTHING FACTOR

From the discussion above, the reader will have gathered that the decision on the most appropriate smoothing factor depends on trial and error. For demand patterns that show a marked upward or downward trend, the smoothing factor that is optimal will tend to be high (0.5 to 0.9), but for relatively level or constant trends, a factor of 0.1 or 0.2 may be best. In practice, with many hundreds or thousands of

TABLE 2–4. PERIOD-TO-PERIOD DEMAND FORECAST BASED ON EXPONENTIAL SMOOTHING, WITH A SMOOTHING FACTOR OF 0.8

a	b	c	d	e	f
Time Period	Actual Demand, in Units	Weighted Actual Demand, b × 0.8, in Units	Weighted Old Forecast, e × 0.2, in Units	New Forecast, c + d, in Units	Amount by Which Forecast Is High (+) or Low (−), e of Prior Row Minus b of Current Row, in Units
prior	—	—	—	(70)	—
1	80	64	14	78	−10
2	90	72	16	88	−12
3	110	88	17	105	−22
4	95	76	21	97	+10
5	105	84	19	103	−8
6	120	96	21	117	−17
7	105	84	23	107	+12
8	130	104	21	125	−23
9	125	100	25	125	0
10	135	108	25	133	−10
Total	1,095	876	202	1,078	124
Average	110	88	20	108	12*

* Mean absolute deviation (MAD).

product items to be put on demand anticipation, the following approach is used:

1. Select a sufficient number of time periods to be representative and thus provide good indications of actual demand patterns.

2. Perform analyses such as in Tables 2–1 to 2–4, but using a computer in lieu of manual methods.

3. Select that smoothing factor for each product or product group that gives the best fit in terms of lowest mean absolute deviation (MAD).

The smoothing factor thus determined is used in practical applications to predict sales demand from period to period.

INTROSPECTIVE SIMULATION

Because of the tremendous amount of data to be analyzed, it is apparent that the type of calculations shown call for computer application. Although we desire a method of predicting *future* demand, we

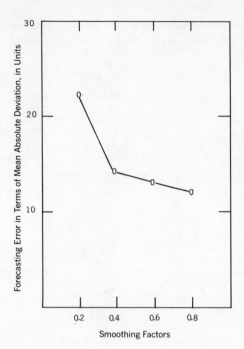

FIGURE 2–2. *Effect of smoothing factor on forecasting error.* In this example, an increase in the smoothing factor resulted in a reduction of the forecasting error—a condition which is usually indicative of strong trends in the data series. In the absence of a marked trend, a factor of 0.1 or 0.2 will often yield the lowest forecast error. Factors can never be less than 0 nor greater than 1.0.

have begun by an introspective study of *past* demand patterns. Next we have "simulated" (or imitated) the real world by looking at these past patterns and examining how various smoothing factors would have worked if they had been used. The objective is to isolate and choose the best factor. Simulation is thus an application of hindsight as a guide to foresight. Our eyes are very much on anticipating the future, but we have looked intensively at the past in order to gain the proper insights into the workings of demand patterns and what these mean for the future.

This application of introspective simulation is but another of the many interesting, useful, and valuable computer simulations which are finding profitable employment in increasing measure throughout various segments of industry.

CONTROL WITH THE TRACKING RATIO

Management utilizes exponential smoothing when the number of product items involved is so large that an automated approach is needed. Having delegated these sales-anticipatory activities to the computer, however, we must next consider the question of control. Certainly, situations will arise that require the executive's attention. Among these are sudden shifts in demand: perhaps a substitute product is gaining ascendancy, or a competitor has a special campaign, or there is a change in consumer tastes and preferences, or a promotional campaign of our own is yielding unexpected results.

The system thus must incorporate a self-monitoring device, which constantly compares forecast with actual demand and which notes a *significant* shift in the actual series. A criterion for evaluating such fluctuations is the *tracking ratio,* which is determined as shown in Table 2–5 (p. 17). From studies similar to those discussed, management decides on a critical value for the tracking ratio. For example, it may be decided that once the tracking ratio reaches −4 or less or +4 or more, a definite shift in demand patterns has occurred. In turn, products or product lines on which a tracking ratio has fallen outside these ±4 control limits call for management attention, review, consideration, and appropriate remedial measures.

TECHNICAL NOTES

A few brief technical comments may be appropriate at this point. First, there may be dissatisfaction with the fact that the exponential-smoothing approach, even at its best, does not show very close agreement with actuality. Such problems will also arise in practice, but there is always the availability of more refined forecasting methods, such as *double smoothing* or *triple smoothing.*

Second, the term *exponential smoothing* will now be explained. "Smoothing" refers to the fact that each forecast really represents an "averaging out" of past experience, based on the weighting of past actual demand and of forecasts. In general, the forecast series will look smoother than the actual demand pattern (see, for example, Figure 2–1). For the word "exponential," we must use some simple algebra, with the symbols D denoting Demand and F indicating Forecast. Subscripts $_1$, $_2$, and so on, refer to periods 1 and 2, while 0 refers to the period prior to period 1. With an α of 0.2, we then have:

$$0.2D_1 + 0.8F_0 = F_1 \qquad \text{(equation 1)}$$
$$0.2D_2 + 0.8F_1 = F_2 \qquad \text{(equation 2)}$$

Note that D_2 is the demand in period 2, while F_2 is the forecast in period 2 of the demand expected for period 3. Similarly, F_1 is the forecast in period 1 of the demand to be expected for period 2.

Now, we substitute the left-hand side of equation 1 for F_1 in equation 2, and obtain:

$$0.2D_2 + 0.8(0.2D_1 + 0.8F_0) = F_2 \qquad \text{(equation 3)}$$

which reduces to

$$0.2(D_2 + 0.8D_1) + (0.8)^2F_0 = F_2 \qquad \text{(equation 4)}$$

Moreover, it is easily seen that as the subscript of F to the right-hand side goes to 3, 4, and 5, the power of 0.8 to the left of F_0 increases to 3, 4, and 5. Thus, an exponent is operating. The successive powers mean that as the exponent is increasing, the effect of 0.8 is decreasing. In other words, with increasing time over successive periods, the effect of the earlier forecasts diminishes exponentially.

SUMMARY

Exponential smoothing is a simple and often highly effective method for anticipating demand from period to period, based on a system that relies heavily on computerized operations. Although errors in forecasting are probable, at least to a small degree, this does not mean that underestimates of demand will result in an inability to service customers, since a company will usually provide for a reserve stock in relation to average expected error. Self-monitoring is accomplished by means of a tracking ratio, which trips a signal when critical control limits are exceeded by the ratio. Detailed management attention is thus required in only those instances where a particular product or product group is experiencing a sharp shift in demand patterns. While exponential smoothing is highly suitable for expectations from one period to the next, it is unlikely to be of value for long-range forecasting.

Exponential smoothing, it will have been noted, is completely introspective in the sense that we look backwards into the time series. From this review of the past, we develop by entirely mechanical means a closely related forecast for the immediately following period. It is apparent that for many purposes we may need a more sophisticated approach, one that permits inclusion of many factors and lends itself readily to more extended predictions. Thus, while exponential smoothing can be a very useful technique, other methods may be needed, depending upon individual requirements.

TABLE 2–5. TRACKING CONTROL OF ACTUAL DEMAND
VERSUS FORECAST DEMAND

a	b	c	d	e	f	g	h
Time Period	Actual Current Demand, in Units	Forecast for Current Period, in Units	Forecast Error, c − b, in Units	Cumulative Forecast Error,* in Units	Cumulative Absolute Deviation,† in Units	Mean Absolute Deviation,‡ in Units	Tracking Ratio,§ e/g
1	100	120	+20	+20	20	20	+1.0
2	150	110	−40	−20	60	30	−0.67
3	70	130	+60	+40	120	40	1.0
4	180	100	−80	−40	200	50	−0.8
5	200	140	(−60	−100	260	52	−2.0

* The cumulative forecast error is found from column d. For period 1, d = e = 20 units. For period 2, we must subtract 40 units from 20 in e, giving a new e of −20. In period 3, we had an error of +60, which, added to the −20 in e, gives a new e of +40, and so on.

† The cumulative absolute deviation is found by cumulating column d without regard to signs, that is, considering negatives as pluses. For period 1, we again have 20. For period 2, we add 40, giving 20 + 40 = 60. For period 3, we add 60, giving 60 + 60 = 120. For period 4, we add 80, giving 120 + 80 = 200.

‡ The mean absolute deviation is the entry in f divided by the number of individual errors in d that comprise each such entry. For example, the first entry in f is 20. It was obtained from the 20 in d. This is just one value, so 20/1 = 20. For period 2, the 60 in f is comprised of two entries, 20 and 40. So we obtain 60/2 = 30. For period 3, 120 is the result of 20 + 40 + 60, or 3 entries, giving 120/3 = 40.

§ The tracking ratio shows the extent to which the forecast is in excess (+) or behind (−) actual volume of demand, based on the ratio of cumulative forecast error to mean absolute deviation. When the ratio exceeds a critical level, a significant change in demand patterns has occurred, requiring review and probably also revision of the forecasting method.

CHAPTER 3

Appraising Long-Term Trends

In the continuing "create-make-market" operations of a business geared to our age of increasingly diversified and sophisticated industrial and consumer products, the demand for formal planning comes strongly to the forefront. Such planning calls for sound methods of intermediate-range and long-term forecasting of market demand, the availability of materials, equipment, and human resources, and related economic, social, and business factors. Exponential smoothing, so practical in the anticipation of short-term demand from month to month, from quarter to quarter, or for similarly limited periods, will usually be inadequate to deal with long-term expectations.

THE COMPUTED TREND LINE

For the long range, a useful analytical tool is the *computed trend line*. Fitted to past years' actual data, the line is then extended to future years. Experience and judgment, properly exercised by management to temper, modify, and adjust the mechanical extrapolations, will lead to the type of forecast that can serve in planning.

Fallibility, which attends all human endeavors, comes to our particular awareness in attempting to make forecasts. In retrospect, all forecasts prove wrong at least to some extent. But forecast we must, if we are to make decisions in a strategy-conscious, planning-oriented, and crisis-avoiding atmosphere of operations. Thus, despite the shortcomings in forecasting, experience proves over and over again that a systematic approach toward planning with a view to the future, in an organized and quantitatively supported manner, will generally be essential to the orderly growth of any business firm.

ILLUSTRATIVE EXAMPLE

As has been pointed out, long-range forecasting involves a combination of mathematical analysis and managerial judgment. The mechanical parts of the analysis can be illustrated quite readily. For the judgmental aspects, however, we need the experienced manager, the marketing specialist, and other staff people who can be aided but never replaced by the quantitative computations.

Let us look at the mathematical analysis first, utilizing the data in the first two columns of Table 3–1 (p. 20). A new product has been marketed by the firm for the past 7 years, and annual sales volume has risen from 100 to 900 units in this period. After examining the graph in Figure 3–1 (p. 21), the sales manager optimistically predicted a volume of 1,100 units for the following year and somewhere between 1,300 and 1,400 units for the subsequent year. As we shall see, this type of "rough and ready" judgment can be quite erroneous. Thoughtful planning should be based on more solid footing, particulary if commitments for additional raw materials, production equipment, warehousing facilities, and distribution channeling must begin well in advance of the eventual new sales volumes.

FITTING THE TREND LINE

Foresight begins with hindsight. As a first step toward forecasting, therefore, we examine past sales volume and draw a line that best fits all the data points. Table 3–1 demonstrates the steps.

1. For the 7 years (column a), the corresponding sales volume in 100's of units (column b) totals to 35.

2. Next, as a convenience for subsequent computations, we show the years in column a in terms of their distance from the central year (column c). Thus, year 4 is central to the series; year 3 is -1, signifying that it is a year earlier, and year 5 is $+1$, indicating that it is a year later.

3. Then we perform the calculations of cross-products (column d) and squared years (column e). For example, $1 \times -3 = -3$, $4 \times -2 = -8$, and so on; and next the square of -3 is $(-3) \times (-3) = 9$, while the square of -2 is 4. Note the totals of 26 and 28 for columns d and e.

TABLE 3-1. CALCULATION OF TREND LINE

a	b	c	d	e
Years Since Product Was Introduced	Sales Volume, in 100's of Units	Years from Central Year*	Cross-Product, $b \times c$	Squared Years, $c \times c$
1	1	−3	−3	9
2	4	−2	−8	4
3	6	−1	−6	1
4	5	0	0	0
5	4	+1	4	1
6	6	+2	12	4
7	9	+3	27	9
Total	35	0	26	28

* With year 4 as central in the span from year 1 to year 7, year 3 is −1 in relation to 4; year 5 is +1; and so on.

FURTHER STEPS

1. The slope of the trend line represents the rate at which the line increases (or decreases). It is found from:

$$\text{Slope} = \text{(Cross-Products Total)}/\text{(Squared-Years Total)}$$
$$= 26/28 = 1.0 \text{ (rounded)}$$

Since the slope is not negative, it increases. The 1.0 signifies that for each successive year, the average rise in sales volume is 1 in terms of the units in column b. Since the units are in 100's, sales volume has increased by an average of 100 units per year.

2. The pivot on which the trend line rests occurs in the year that corresponds to 0 in column c. This is year 4. How high is the pivot located? We find:

$$\text{Pivot} = \text{(Total of Sales Volumes)}/\text{(No. of Years)}$$
$$= 35/7 = 5, \text{ or } 500 \text{ units}$$

Coincidentally, this point happens to coincide with the actual sales in year 4.

RESULT

The trend line is 5 for year 4. For each successive subsequent year the trend line rises by 1.0 per year, and for each year prior to year 4 it is 1.0 lower (as drawn on the sales-volume diagram).

4. The slope of the line of best fit is now found from the ratio of the cross-products total to the squared-years total, giving 26/28 or 1.0 (rounded). The slope is positive, thus indicating that the line is ascending from left to right. A negative slope would have signified a declining trend.

5. The pivot is the level at which the slope rests. It is found by dividing the total sales volume for the 7 years, 35, by 7, giving 5 in 100's of units.

Now we are ready to draw the line of best fit, or trend line, to the

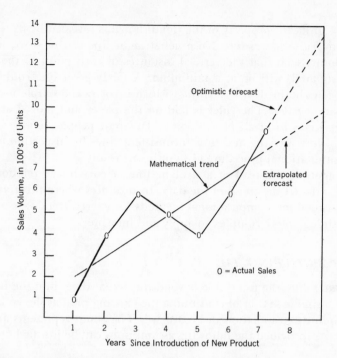

FIGURE 3–1. *Trend line for sales volume*. From the 7 years of actual sales experience, a trend line has been computed. By extending, or extrapolating, this line, a mathematical prediction is obtained. Such a prediction need not agree with other predictions, which may be either more optimistic or more pessimistic, depending upon knowledge of other market factors and portents.

data. We start at the point corresponding to the central year, 4, and go upward to a sales volume of 5 units in 100's. This establishes the pivot point, which coincidentally also happens to be the actual sales volume (but need not be such). In the next year, 5, the sales trend should be up by 1.0 unit, since the latter figure represents the slope of the line. Thus, the trend should be at 6 units for year 5, at 7 units for year 6, and at 8 units for year 7. Going back in time, we see that year 3 should now be 1.0 unit below the 5 units of the pivot year, giving 4 units, with a level of 2 units by the time we have gone back to year 1. Connecting these points, we obtain the mathematical trend line that best describes the average increase of the 7 years' actual sales volume.

A significant property of the trend shown is revealed by its technical term *least-squares line*. No other straight line can be fitted to the data points such that the vertical distances of each point to the line, when squared, will be at a minimum. A fairly good line could also have been obtained by *eye-balling*, which involves the simple use of a transparent ruler. The ruler is laid on the paper and moved around until it seems to fit all of the points. Different people, however, will tend to draw varying and thus inconsistent lines by inspection, while the computational procedure gives only one result.

Sometimes, instead of a straight line, a curvilinear relationship will best depict the trend in the data. In instances where this relationship is called for, computational methods for curved trends are available, although more complex to apply and interpret.

EXTRAPOLATING THE TREND LINE

Extending the trend line beyond the actual data, into the future, is now a simple matter of continuing the existing plot, as shown by the broken-line extrapolation in Figure 3–1. The result represents a valid "forecast," provided the following assumptions can be justified:

1. The computed trend relationship is an accurate description of the many historical forces producing the trend line.
2. There is good reason to expect that these forces will continue to behave in essentially the same way as in the past.
3. No new factors are expected to operate that would tend to significantly modify, alter, or otherwise disturb the projected trend.

To the degree that these assumptions are affected by foreseeable changes in conditions, as envisioned by management and staff people, modifications in the forecast will be required. The mathematical projection is thus merely a starting point and not the end result of the forecasting activity.

For the illustrative case history, there existed a rather optimistic forecast prepared by the sales manager on the basis of recent experience (the past 3 years). He envisioned continuing prosperity and other market factors that would be beneficial to the sale of this particular item. But when the sales manager saw the mathematical trend, he became more cautious. He recognized that a few years earlier there had been a general recession in the economy, and thus part of the more recent strong buildup was merely a "catching up" with the earlier depressed sales volume of year 5. After several discussions among executives and staff people, a more modest anticipation than the original optimistic estimate, but higher than the purely mathematical extrapolation, was adopted as *the* forecast on which to base planning.

EXTENDED USES OF THE TREND LINE

Similar forecasts were prepared for all of the major products marketed by the firm in the illustrative example. The procedures shown are just as valid for old items, which have been part of the product line for decades, as they are for new items. It is often found, however, that many old products have a declining trend. When such downward tendencies are marked, they may well point to the desirability of either dropping the item or else seeking innovation—in terms of design and redesign or new marketing approaches—with a view toward trend reversal. Thus a forecast, by the very fact of its existence, may give rise to management actions that will then prove the initial projection to be superseded.

DETERMINING THE PROPER AMOUNT
OF HISTORICAL DATA

For the illustrative example, the time period of 7 years used in calculating the trend line represented the total life span of the new product to date. Life span is, however, not a generally applicable criterion for the amount of historical sales data to be utilized. A more widely recognized rule is that the trend should be computed from those historical data thought to represent most closely the forces that are likely to continue operating in the future.

Unfortunately, there are few guidelines for ascertaining positively that certain economic, industrial, and marketing factors prevailing in a given historical period will continue in the future. The following guidelines may be of service in making a decision:

1. Generally, the more recent the historical data, the more pertinent they are likely to be at least for the near future.
2. The rule in guideline 1 can be misleading if a cycle is evident in the past data, because a 2- or 3-year cycle may be misinterpreted as a long-term trend. Assume that a cycle goes upward for about 2 years and then swings downward for the next 2 years. It would be erroneous

to extrapolate an upward swing beyond its normal time span. For example, the data in Figure 3–1 reveal a cycle. If we had merely used the last 2 years of the upward swing (regardless of whether a free-hand or computed trend is drawn), then the trend-line extrapolation would have tended to shoot upward, as indicated by the broken line labeled "Optimistic Forecast." Such optimism is, however, not likely to be warranted in view of the cyclical pattern evidenced. As a further example, in year 5 it would have been erroneous to assume from the 2 years immediately preceding that a long-term downward trend was operating.

3. Data from at least the past 20 years, if available, should be examined to ascertain whether or not cyclical variations are present.

4. The existence of a cycle in historical data need not mean that the cycle will persist, particularly if strong innovative forces are at work. As an example, for decades many countries throughout the world have been experiencing a 2- to 3-year "textile cycle." But in recent history, that cycle has disappeared. Technological innovations— such as new fiber blends, stretch fabrics, wash-and-wear materials, permanent-press synthetics, stain-resistant finishes, and outdoor carpeting —have swept away the old demand patterns. Changes in established patterns are occurring more frequently, rapidly, and radically than ever before in an economy geared to innovation.

5. Although 20 years' data may be examined to note whether or not a series contains cyclical variations, it is probably not desirable to include more than 15 years in calculating a historical trend. Data older than 15 years are likely to be outdated. Similarly, the use of only 5 years may be questionable as probably not including all factors at work in a series. Therefore, a broad and general rule for a starting-point analysis would put a 10-year period as the most suitable for trend calculations.

6. In the determination of the proper time period, thought should also be given to the possibility that a curvilinear trend may be operative, and the data should be viewed in this light.

Finally, not only the choice of the amount of historical data to include in the trend calculation, but practically all aspects of forecasting depend on close interchange of information and opinions between those people in the organization concerned with trend calculation and those responsible for appraising market factors and related developments that are deemed significant in evaluating future prospects.

SUMMARY

Effective planning hinges on forecasts of expected business conditions. Long-term trend determinations, projected for the applicable planning period and based on a combination of mathematically supported analysis and executive-managerial judgment, are the only basis on which sound decisions and actions for the future can be founded.

CHAPTER 4

Plotting Percentage Projections

A growing economy, combined with an apparently self-accelerating pace of progress in science and technology, can bring special rewards to the innovator. New products and ventures, if properly conceived and managed, will yield good rates of annual sales buildup. Volume, in such instances, does not merely rise in terms of a fixed amount from one year to the next. In addition, there will often be a percentage boost: A given percentage of growth applies to successively larger totals from year to year. As a result, an annual growth rate of 40 per cent can lead to a tenfold expansion in the span of 8 years.

THE PERCENTAGE CHART

Growth in value, sales, or other data that occurs in percentage terms from one period to the next, may be advantageously plotted on a chart, as in Figure 4–1, where the vertical scale is in percentage increments. The reader can easily verify that, for example, the distance from 100 to 150, from 200 to 300, and from 400 to 600, all representing jumps of 50 per cent, are indeed of identical length on the scale.

The trend line indicates a growth in sales volume of 40 per cent each year. Thus, $100 rises to $140 in year 2; next, 40 per cent applied to this sum gives a new total of $196; and so on, until $1,054 is reached for year 8. The figure for the final year and for the preceding one is obtained by linear extension of the trend line. The value of the percentage chart thus becomes clear: A constant percentage rate of growth appears in linear form. Compare this result with the curved trend line under ordinary scaling in Figure 4–2 (p. 28) for the same data. The percentage chart also permits a more balanced comparison of actual versus trend values for the successive years. With an ordinary chart, if

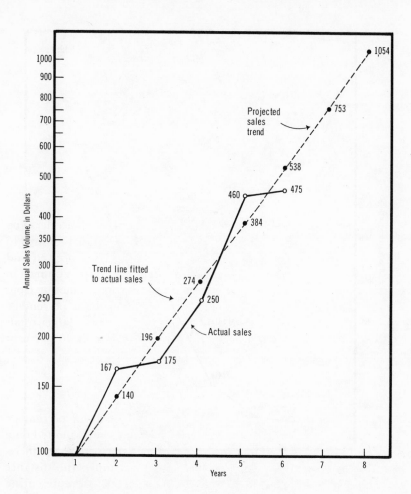

FIGURE 4–1. *Growth curve, percentage-chart plot.* From the trend of actual sales, a growth line of 40 per cent is inferred. The projection shows expected sales for the next 2 years provided past growth rates continue. When a constant percentage gain is expected, such as 40 per cent in this example, then a percentage scale results in a straight-line trend, as shown by the broken line.

percentage increments are involved, earlier years will appear to deviate less from the trend line while later years will appear to deviate more.

Plotting Percentage Projections   27

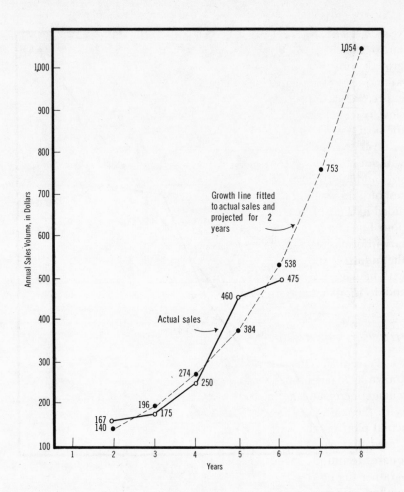

FIGURE 4–2. *Growth curve, plot of actual sales with trend.* Unlike the percentage chart (see Figure 4–1), the graph here does not permit a straight-line projection of the trend.

INTERPRETING THE CHART

What does the chart indicate with regard to future expectations? A review of the actual sales plotted would tend to give the first-glance impression that sales are beginning to level off near the $500 volume. The straight-line trend extrapolation, however, predicts further substantial gains, warranting the expectation of doubling volume within 2 years. Looking back on the chart, we note a slow period of sales, similar to years 5 and 6, for the progress from year 2 to year 3. This slow growth coincided with a cyclical low for the industry, but the losses were quickly recuperated in years 4 and 5. A parallel development is expected for the future. Although the year just completed has been slow, corresponding to an industrywide lull, all indications are that in the next 2 years we will recoup our long-term growth rate.

While these factors and relationships could have been brought out without charting, the value of the percentage chart is that it emphasizes and highlights this pattern. Executives, managers, and staff people responsible for forecasting and for factual support of decisions are thus aided in their judgment, evaluation, and final choice of a course of action. The quantitative relationships provided by the chart; supplementary information, such as on general cycles and trends in the economy, the industry, and the market; plus qualitative information, combined with managerial experience and judgment—all go into the forecasting and decision-making process.

HINTS ON PREPARING PERCENTAGE CHARTS

Percentage charts can be drawn easily on special graph paper, known as logarithmic, or log, paper. It so happens that constant-percentage increments are characteristic of the progression of logarithms. With the ruling of the graph built on the basis of log increments for actual plotting, the scales are simply used as we have done. It has been hinted that trend lines can also be computed by means of the least-squares technique given in Chapter 3. If this more precise approach —rather than a free-hand approximation—is desired, the least-squares method will work readily, provided the data on sales volume are expressed as logarithms.

REPURCHASE PERCENTAGES

It should be emphasized that it is not sufficient for a series to exhibit "percentage characteristics" to result in a straight-line trend. What is important is that each successive increment of growth occurs at a constant percentage of the preceding total. An interesting marketing phenomenon, in which percentages work differently from the way just discussed, relates to the value of new customer acquisitions (see Fig. 4–3, p. 30). Assume, for example, that market research has shown a

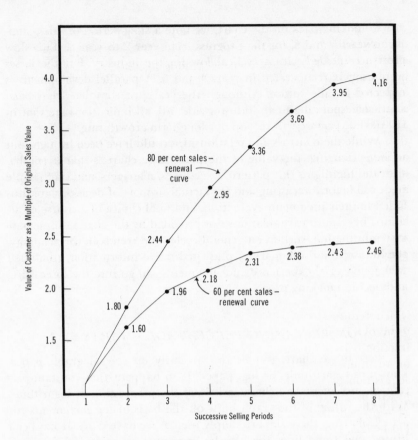

FIGURE 4–3. *Value of a customer acquisition.* If the rate of renewal of sale (repurchase of item, renewal of subscription or club membership) is 60 per cent, then $1.00 earned in the initial period will grow to $1.00 + 0.6 = $1.60 in period 2, and to $1.60 + (0.6 × 0.6) = $1.96 in period 3. While all curves flatten out eventually, the desirability of a high renewal rate is emphasized by this analysis. Leveling out of the 60 and 80 per cent curves will be at $2\frac{1}{2}$ and 5 times the initial sales value. For a curve of 70 per cent renewals, leveling would be reached at $3\frac{1}{3}$ times the initial sales value.

likelihood that 60 per cent of newly gained customers will repurchase the item in the next period. Thus, each dollar gained in the initial period will grow to $1 + (0.6 × $1) = $1.60 by period 2, to $1.60 + (0.6 × 0.6 × $1) = $1.96 in period 3, and to $2.44 in period 8. On the other hand, if there is a renewal rate of 80 per cent, the dollar will be worth $4.16 by period 8.

Admittedly, this illustration ignores the effect of interest rates over extended periods of time. It does, however, pinpoint the value of efforts to retain customers by predicting the total gain attainable. The graph is particularly important when a firm seeks to justify advertising and promotional expenditures. For example, a program was almost scuttled because a $120,000 promotion was expected to yield merely $100,000 of profit from initial new sales. It was pointed out, however, that by the end of period 2, sales profit would have reached $160,000 and eventually would be $250,000. The extended-profit analysis demonstrates the program to be well worth while, even after allowance is made for various risk factors, contingencies, and interest expense.

Some readers may be interested in a simple mathematical formulation of the repurchase-percentage determinations. If we let p represent the fraction of customers who repurchase an item in the next period, with V_n as the value of a customer acquisition after n periods, then:

$$V_n = 1 + p + p^2 + \ldots p^{n-1}$$

which reduces to $(1 - p^n) / (1 - p)$. This is the familiar sum of n terms of a geometric progression with initial value 1, p being a decimal fraction between 0 and 1, and n representing an integer 1, 2, 3, and so on to infinity. When n does reach infinity, the value of a customer acquisition becomes $1/(1 - p)$. For example, for $p = 0.6$, at infinity, p^n will be zero (a fraction raised to an infinite power is always zero); $(1 - p^n)$ will then be 1.0; and V_n will be $1/(1 - p) = 1/(1 - 0.6) = 1/0.4 = 2.5$.

SUMMARY

Charts based on percentage growth rates are of considerable value to marketing and sales management. Actual sales can be compared with past growth rates, giving due account to both long-term trends and cyclical fluctuations. A projection of these trends, combined with good judgment in evaluating qualitative and quantitative factors affecting future developments, can lead to highly useful forecasts. In turn, decisions on advertising and promotional strategy and provision of merchandise to meet anticipated demand are facilitated.

Author's note: John G. I. Mackay, of the Dominion Bureau of Statistics, Socio-Economic Statistics Branch, Ottawa, Ontario, Canada, made several helpful suggestions which have been incorporated in this chapter.

Allowing for Seasonal Variation

Long-term trends and cyclical fluctuations are considered prominently in predicting the total volume for the coming year. However, allowances must be made for seasonal variations—the weeks or months of peaks and troughs in customer demand within the year. Fortunately, seasonal variation is generally a relatively predictable portion of a time series.

A TYPICAL SEASONAL PATTERN

An illustration of seasonal variation, involving two periods of peak volume within a year, is shown in Figure 5–1, which is based on data in Table 5–1 (p. 34). Despite evidence of a strong trend and cycle, represented by the annual totals of 600, 480, 960, and 840 for the 4 years, the pattern within each year is relatively stable. We note a peak in May and another one in October or November. Both of the latter months are relatively high, and the slight differences were found ascribable to timing of advertising.

By plotting the data in terms of percentages, with each month as a percentage of the year's average (total volume divided by 12), we obtain Figure 5–2 (p. 35), which reveals an interesting item of further insight. During 1966, the company experienced less marked seasonal fluctuations than in prior years. Management felt that this occurrence was caused by special circumstances, which were not likely to be experienced in the same magnitude in 1967. Some degree of gradual dampening of seasonal peaks and troughs was, however, expected.

After further studies and discussions, it was believed that an average of the seasonal patterns for the past 4 years would reflect the typical situation likely to prevail in the coming year. Shown as the "Average" column in Table 5–1, it is plotted to the left in Figure 5–3 (p. 36).

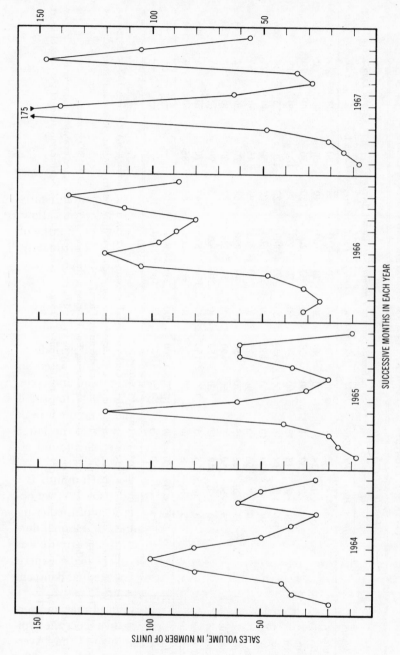

FIGURE 5–1. *Plot of actual sales*. A seasonal pattern is revealed, with peaks in May–June and October–November.

33

TABLE 5-1. MONTHLY SALES WITH RANGE OF VARIATION AND CONTROL LIMITS

Month	Monthly Sales, Number of Units*				Monthly Sales as Percentage of Annual Average†							Control Limits, Per Cent§		
	1964	1965	1966	1967	1964	1965	1966	1967	Total	Average	Range‡	±	Lower	Upper
January	20	8	32	7	40	20	40	10	110	28	30	24	4	52
February	35	16	24	14	70	40	30	20	160	40	50	40	0	80
March	40	20	32	21	80	50	40	30	200	50	50	40	10	90
April	80	40	48	49	160	100	60	70	390	98	100	80	18	178
May	100	120	104	175	200	300	130	250	880	220	170	136	84	356
June	80	60	120	140	160	150	150	200	660	165	50	40	125	205
July	50	30	96	63	100	75	120	90	385	96	45	36	60	132
August	35	20	88	28	70	50	110	40	270	68	70	56	12	124
September	25	36	80	35	50	90	100	50	290	72	50	40	32	112
October	60	60	112	147	120	150	140	210	620	155	90	72	83	227
November	50	60	136	105	100	150	170	150	570	142	70	56	86	198
December	25	10	88	56	50	25	110	80	265	66	85	68	0	134
Total	600	480	960	840	1,200	1,200	1,200	1,200	4,800	1,200	—	—	—	—
Average	50	40	80	70	100	100	100	100	100	100	—	—	—	—

* Monthly units sold represent the past pattern of volume.

† The sales are next expressed as a percentage of the annual average. For example, 20 units in January of 1964 gives 100 × 20/50 = 40 per cent. When totaled, these percentages yield the typical experience for each month in relative terms. Seasonal factors are thus identified. Thus in January, sales are typically 28 per cent of the annual total.

‡ Range is the difference between highest and lowest value. For February, the range is 70 − 20 = 50 per cent.

§ Control limits are based on the annual average and apply to monthly percentages. For March, for example, the average is 50 per cent. Applying the control limit of ±40 per cent gives an upper limit of 90 and a lower limit of 10. The determination of the control limit is shown in Table 5-2.

34

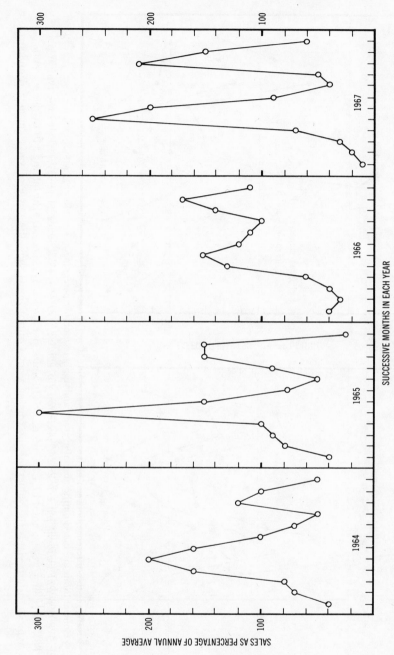

FIGURE 5–2. *Monthly sales as percentage of annual average.* The average is 100 per cent. Each year's sales are thus on the same basis, regardless of the effect of trends and cycles on the actual annual total.

35

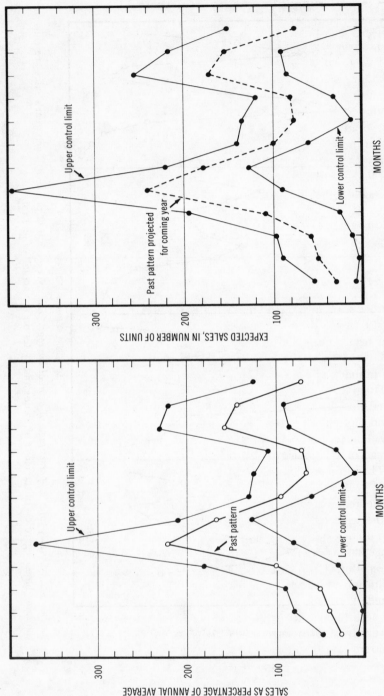

FIGURE 5–3. *Typical seasonal pattern and expectation for coming year.* Past experience (4 years) revealed the typical pattern. For the coming year, a total of 1,320 units, or 110 units, per month, is expected. Multiplying 110 by the percentages of the typical pattern yields the values for the coming year. Control limits show the range of variation at a confidence level of 90 per cent.

SETTING THE CONTROL LIMITS

A special feature of the plot of typical seasonal pattern is the set of upper and lower control limits. The values so described define a confidence level of 90 per cent. In other words, 90 per cent of the time, the actual pattern should fall within these limits. From Table 5–1, it is noted that the confidence limits are based on past variations in percentage of sales volume, expressed in terms of the "Range." For example, January volume was 40, 20, 40, and 10 per cent of the annual average for each of the 4 years. The highest value, 40, minus the lowest value, 10, yields a range of 30. Next, this range is multiplied by a probability factor of 0.8, to yield a control limit of ±24 above and below the average of 28. The upper control limit thus becomes 52; the lower control limit is 4.

The factor 0.8 is based on statistical calculations involving the normal-probability curve, discussed in Table 5–2 (p. 38).

PROJECTING THE SEASONAL PATTERN

All that remains to be done is to project the typical seasonal effect in the past to the future year. Assume that a total volume of 1,320 units has been forecast, so that the monthly average is one-twelfth of this, or 110.

For January, applying the typical past-experience value of 28 per cent to 110 gives 31 units. For February, 40 per cent × 110 = 44 units. Calculated thus for all months, the pattern expected for next year is found and plotted to the right of Figure 5–3. Control limits are found similarly. For January we apply the control-limit percentage ±24 to the average of 110, giving ±26 units. For January, 31 units are predicted. Therefore, the upper limit is 31 + 26 = 52, while the lower limit at 31 − 52 is set at 4.

As the year progresses, we will plot the actual volume of sales against the expected pattern. So long as the deviations (which are bound to occur) stay within the control limits, we know that no serious change has occurred. Actual sales are within the expected range of fluctuation. But, if a control limit is exceeded by actual sales volume, there is an indication that total business will probably be better than anticipated. Appropriate action by management may be taken, such as ordering additional production to meet the demand that is building up. Conversely, if actual volume falls below the lower control limit, then a retrenchment may need to be considered, to avert being stuck

TABLE 5–2. CONTROL-LIMIT FACTORS F_c

Number of Years (or Other Time Periods) Used to Determine Each Range	Confidence Level, Per Cent†				
	95	90	80 or	70	50
	Risk of Error, Per Cent*				
	5	10	20	30	50
2	1.8‡	1.5	1.1	0.9	0.6
3	1.2	1.0	0.8	0.6	0.4
4	1.0	0.8	0.6	0.5	0.3
5	0.8	0.7	0.6	0.4	0.3
6	0.8	0.6	0.5	0.4	0.3
8	0.7	0.6	0.5	0.4	0.2
10	0.6	0.5	0.4	0.3	0.2

* Risk of error is the probability, as a per cent, that an actual monthly (or other period) sales value will fall outside the upper or lower control limit as a result of chance fluctuations alone, and no real change in total annual sales to be anticipated has occurred.

† Confidence level, as a per cent, is thus 100 per cent minus risk of error.

‡ Factors F_c are used as follows to find control limits: Assume that management is willing to incur a risk of error of 10 per cent, so that the confidence level chosen is 90 per cent, and that for the past 4 years the sales in one month have averaged to 50 per cent of the anticipated total. Also, the range based on these 4 years is 40 per cent. Then:

$$\text{Control Limits} = \text{Average} \pm \text{Range} \times F_c$$
$$= 50 \pm 40 \times 0.8$$
$$= 50 \pm 32, \text{ or } 18 \text{ and } 82$$

The last two values, 18 and 82, are the lower and upper control limits as a per cent.

SOURCE: Factors F_c are based on the well-known coefficients d_2, due to L. H. C. Tippett, for converting ranges to a measure of variability known as "Standard Deviation" and an assumption that, ordinarily, sales-volume variations will be distributed according to the normal-curve law. For a further discussion see, for example, N. L. Enrick, *Quality Control and Reliability* (5th ed.; New York: Industrial Press, 1966), Chap. 15.

with unsold merchandise at the end of the season. The *exception principle* of management is thus operational. Only in those instances where it is needed will executive time be called for to review and revise prior forecasts and decisions.

It should further be emphasized that it may be a simple matter for management to control several product items without an elaborate mechanism of seasonal-pattern forecasting with control limits. If a company has a large variety of items, however, it is highly desirable to rely on procedures which relieve management of needless routines.

CHAPTER 5

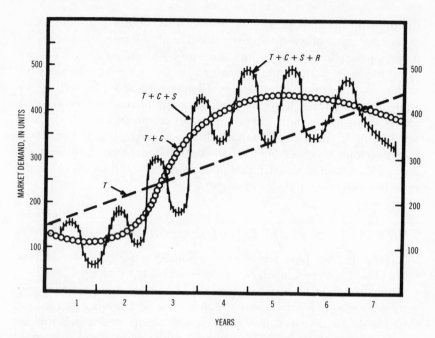

FIGURE 5–4. *Components of a time series.* Trend *T*, Cycle *C*, Seasonal *S*, and Random fluctuations *R* together are the structural factors producing an observed series of business data over time.

The system provided here accomplishes this purpose, thus giving executives more time to deal with other matters of significance.

RELATING SEASONAL PATTERN TO TREND AND CYCLE

A business-data series may be looked on as consisting of several components, so that any individual observed point is the result of long-term trend *T*, cyclical fluctuations *C*, seasonal variation *S*, plus irregular and apparently random variability *R*. In formula terms:

$$\text{Any Point} = T + C + S + R$$
$$= \text{Trend} + \text{Cycle} + \text{Seasonal} + \text{Random}$$

These components are illustrated in Figure 5–4.

The method given here utilizes past patterns of seasonal variation in projecting future seasonal patterns. It does not indicate how to predict the year's anticipated total. The latter is evaluated by means of the trend projections previously described as modified by judgment, experience, and other qualitative detail and information known to management. Business-cycle indicators and various published sources of information, such as those provided by various governmental and private organizations (discussed in Chapters 12 and 13), will be of value in anticipating the year's total. Random fluctuations are allowed for by the control limits. These limits, in conjunction with the seasonal pattern, are of considerable value to management. If the actual sales developments veer beyond the control limits that have been set around the seasonal pattern, this occurrence may well signal the need to review and revise the year's forecast.

THE VALUE OF PLANNING FOR SEASONAL VARIATION

Thus far, we have dealt with seasonal variation on an annual basis. Often, however, it will be found desirable to break up a year into two or more parts, corresponding to the two or more seasons that will yield peak sales or other business volume. Instead of making forecasts of sales for the total year, it may be preferable to develop such anticipations for each season total. Also, instead of developing and preparing graphs on a month-by-month basis, it is often advantageous to compute and plot these data cumulatively. Examples of cumulative seasonal charts and corresponding control limits are given elsewhere.[1]

It may be asked why we are concerned with seasonal variation. Why not just produce to demand as it arises? The answer is that scarcely a firm exists which can afford to take such a position. Unless seasonal needs can be anticipated, the firm is unable to plan properly for the purchase of goods from suppliers, to produce far enough ahead of schedule to meet customer demand, or to build up inventories in advance of actual need. In fact, the more marked a seasonal variation, the more likely it is that either the supplier or our own plant will be unable to meet demand from current production. Scheduling and planning are therefore essential, which in turn call for good estimates of probable future needs. Improper estimates may result either in inadequate stock and resulting customer dissatisfaction and lost sales or in surpluses that are left over at the end of the season and may have to be sold at "distress prices."

---

[1] Norbert Lloyd Enrick, *Inventory Management: Installation, Operation, and Control* (San Francisco: Chandler Publishing Company, 1968), Chap. 5.

SUMMARY

A systematic means of allowing for expected seasonal variations in demand has been developed in this chapter. The method entails the evaluation of likely seasonal patterns with control limits to allow for the additional factor of randomlike fluctuations. The control charts so developed will be of value wherever a large variety of product items is subject to seasonal peaks and troughs. A relatively good degree of future anticipation and control is attainable.

CHAPTER 6

Simulating Order and Merchandise Flows

Cycles in consumer demand, industrial production, and inventory are but a few of the problems that recur with varying degrees of acuteness in virtually all industries. The problems created by these fluctuations cannot be minimized easily. Modern management science has, however, developed forecasting techniques which aid in anticipating and coping with adverse trends and cycles. A technique of considerable interest for management involves the simulation of the effects of various order and merchandise flows on a computer, known also as *industrial dynamics,* a term coined by Professor Jay W. Forrester of the Massachusetts Institute of Technology. While industrial dynamics can be applied to many areas in economic analysis and business-strategy formulation, the chief interest in this chapter will focus on how variations in consumer demand affect production, inventory, and merchandise flows. From an understanding of these effects, appropriate managerial strategy to lessen the impact of cycles can be developed, such as by anticipating and allowing for them.

SIMULATION METHOD

Business simulation utilizes a digital computer, on which are described the conditions regarding an industry, a company operating within that industry, and the company's markets. On the basis of this information, the computer is then asked to investigate how certain management decisions on marketing method, distribution policy, production functions, or other activities would work out in practice. The computer will usually generate charts showing, over the course of time, the effects of a decision on finances, sales, manpower, product movement, and other factors of interest. After various potential management decisions have been investigated, an optimal strategy can then be adopted in "real life." In a matter of minutes, computer simulation can run through a dozen or more simulated time spans into future months or years. Actual actions taken are then guided by this prior evaluation and the information, insights, cautions, and opportunities revealed.

Some of the questions that can be studied with the aid of simulation, particularly in the sales and marketing areas, are the following:

1. Where and how should promotional expenditures and investments be made to best advantage?

2. What will be the effect of shifting market demands on (a) the industry generally and (b) our firm particularly? How can we best counter any adverse trends revealed?

3. What effects will changes in imports and exports have?

4. Can customer service be improved? How much will better service mean in terms of increased patronage?

5. Are we missing any new product markets? If so, which areas should be studied further?

6. How can we best anticipate demand cycles?

7. Do further market potentials warrant investment in costly new machinery and equipment?

Quite evidently, answers to these questions can directly benefit management in many ways. For example, in one firm a simulation study contributed to a better understanding of the effect of inventory policies. Subsequent changes in existing methods of business operation were successful in leading to better customer service while at the same time increasing the sales-to-inventory ratio of the firm.

Simulation models have been used in a large number of industries, such as oil-tanker construction, lumber, shoe-leather-hides, textile fibers and fabrics, apparel manufacture, and copper smelting.

ILLUSTRATIVE EXAMPLE

In order to demonstrate how simulation is applied, we will examine an industrial example so simplified as to yield to pen-and-paper treatment rather than computer analysis. Problems had arisen in the industry because of what was considered an excessive price markup by the wholesaler. The wholesaler in turn blamed unduly high fluctuation in demand, which forced him to incur the costs of large inventories. A survey revealed these basic factors:

1. The typical retailer keeps an inventory of 10 units of the product involved. At the end of each week, he reorders from the wholesaler to replenish his stock. It takes about 2 weeks to receive this replacement merchandise. Some retailers do not understand why they are occasionally overstocked or understocked since, as one of them put it, "I order exactly what I sell each week," thus reflecting predominant retailer practice in the industry.

2. The typical wholesaler also tries to keep an inventory of about 10 units per dealer served. He fills the retailer's order from this stock. Once a week, he replenishes his stock by ordering from the factory exactly what he shipped to the retailer.

3. There is usually a delay of 1 week from the time that the wholesaler has filled an order until he gets around to (a) assessing his inventory position and (b) then mailing his replenishment order.

4. Once an order arrives at the factory, the merchandise can be produced and shipped within 1 week. It arrives at the wholesaler's the following week.

This sequence of activities and the typical time lags are sketched in Figure 6–1.

We can now simulate the behavior of retailer, wholesaler, and factory over a period of weeks, as in Table 6–1 (p. 46), keeping in mind the time lags noted above. Observe that, for example:

1. Retailer's order received by wholesaler in week 2 *equals* sales in week 1.

2. Orders received at factory in week 4 *equals* orders received by wholesaler in week 2, which *equals* sales in week 1.

Other similar relations are readily gleaned from the tabulation prepared. By knowing the structure of the market system, the delays that arise, and the policies in operation, we can calculate characteristic responses to various market conditions. Demand can be traced from one time period to the next, by moving from week to week in the tabulation.

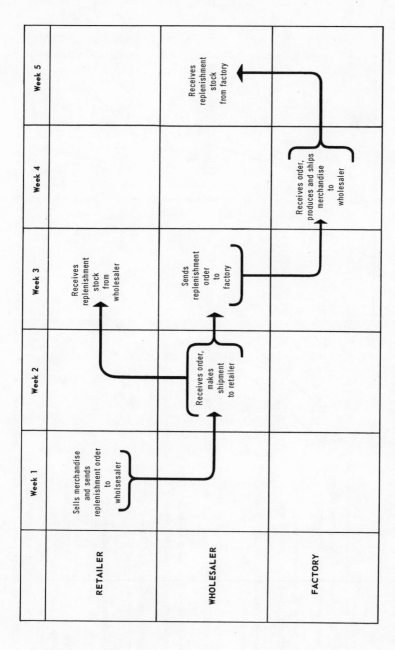

FIGURE 6–1. *Flow of orders and goods.* The particular flow will depend on the structure of an industry, so that the flow depicted here is merely a simplified example.

TABLE 6-1. FLOW OF ORDERS AND GOODS, WITH RESULTANT FLUCTUATIONS IN PRODUCTION AND INVENTORIES

							Successive Weeks							
Action Taken	1	2	3	4	5	6	7	8	9	10	11	12	13	14
							Number of Units							
a. Retailer sells merchandise and sends replenishment order to wholesaler	10	11	12	11	10	9	8	9	10	10	10	10	10	10
b. Order received at wholesaler's and shipment made (1 week after a)	(10)†	10*	11	12	11	10	9	8	9	10	10	10	10	10
c. Goods received by retailer (1 week after b)	(10)	(10)	10	11	12	11	10	9	8	9	10	10	10	10
d. Retailer's inventory, based on 10 units at start ($= 10 + c - a$)	(10)	(9)	7	7	9	11	13	13	11	10	10	10	10	10
e. Wholesaler sends order to factory (1 week after b) to replenish stock	(10)	(10)	10	11	12	11	10	9	8	9	10	10	10	10
f. Factory produces and ships goods (1 week after e)	(10)	(10)	(10)	10	11	12	11	10	9	8	9	10	10	10
g. Goods received by wholesaler (1 week after f)	(10)	(10)	(10)	(10)	10	11	12	11	10	9	8	9	10	10
h. Wholesaler's inventory, based on 10 units at start ($= 10 + g - b$)	(10)	(10)	(9)	(7)	6	7	10	13	14	13	11	10	10	10

* Arrows indicate direction of flow.

† Parentheses denote entries from sales in prior weeks (before week 1) with stable demand at 10 units per week.

SIMULATION RESULTS

The simulation results can best be visualized in graphic form (see Fig. 6–2, p. 48). We observe:

1. The retailer's method of ordering causes him to end up with a *low inventory* when there is *high demand*, and vice versa.

2. A variation of ± 20 per cent in the retailer's sales demand produces a variation of ± 30 per cent in the retailer's inventory and a variation of ± 40 per cent in the wholesaler's inventories.

3. The wholesaler's inventory tends to rise as production decreases, and vice versa.

4. Several periods (weeks) after demand has stabilized, production and inventory levels are still changing.

We can now experiment with the industry structure in an attempt to eliminate or reduce many of these undesirable effects. For example, we might decide to try to speed the order-handling process from retailer to wholesaler to factory. This change can be simulated by reducing the various time lags in the computer model of the industry. When the new simulation run has been completed, we will note whether the changes brought desirable or undesirable results. Other features to experiment with by means of simulation would involve (1) some system for anticipating demand and ordering from the wholesaler and the factory accordingly, (2) various inventory-control policies, and (3) increased production speeds.

This has been a simple illustration; a real-life industry problem is more complex, but the principles of analysis shown here are readily extended for these situations. Work done on a computer will include all graphing.

SUMMARY

Simulation of order and merchandise flows serves as a "time-compression" to the extent of achieving in effect simultaneity. Instead of adopting policies and waiting to see how these policies work themselves out in the real world, we first simulate the future, based on the outcomes of various assumed policies and decisions. From the forecast of this simulated future, an actual decision can be made that is likely to yield optimal results. Simulation, by means of the principles of industrial dynamics, is thus an important predictive tool for marketing and sales management.

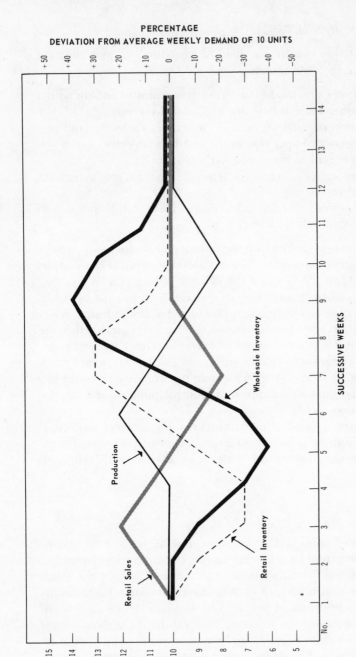

FIGURE 6-2. *Industrial dynamics study.* As a result of variation in sales and of time lags in the flow of orders and goods, production and inventories fluctuate. Often the fluctuations exceed the variation in retail sales. In the example shown here, wholesale inventories fluctuate 40 per cent and retail inventories fluctuate 30 per cent, even though retail sales vary by only 20 per cent.

48

CHAPTER 7

Making a Correlation Analysis

Accomplishing a given sales volume in the marketplace is generally the result of many factors. Some of these, such as type and extent of advertising, promotional programs, and salesmen's calls, are under the firm's control. Others, such as general economic conditions and competitors' actions, are not. Over a period of time, sales experience is accumulated showing the total volume under varying conditions, both within and beyond the firm's control.

DEFINING CORRELATION ANALYSIS

In order to develop future plans and programs in an effective manner, it is highly desirable to understand the relative effect of *each individual variable*—such as amount of advertising, number of salesmen's visits, dollars expended for promotion, total market available—on the total sales volume to be expected for the firm. An expression providing this type of information is the *estimating equation*. When the variables involved are many, the pursuit of such a formula is usually successful with a technique known as *multiple correlation analysis*.

The term "correlation" refers to the relationships among variables, while "multiple" indicates that more than two variables are involved. For only two variables, the expression *simple correlation* applies. In some instances, the phrases *multiple regression* or *simple regression* are found in use, but these convey a more restrictive implication: Only the equation of relationship among the variables is desired, omitting criteria of degree of relationship, such as are measured by the *correlation coefficient.*

TABLE 7-1. SALES VOLUME RELATED TO ADVERTISING EXPENDITURES

	a	b	c	d	e	f	g	h	i	j	k	l
	Monthly Sales, in Units, S	Advertising, $100 per Month		Deviations from Each Average*			Squared Deviations			Cross-Products		
		We, W	Competitor, C	$S - \bar{S}$	$W - \bar{W}$	$C - \bar{C}$	d^2	e^2	f^2	$d \times e$	$d \times f$	$e \times f$
Month												
January	44	21	19	−1	1	−1	1	1	1	−1	1	−1
February	60	19	18	15	−1	−2	225	1	4	−15	−30	2
March	30	15	19	−15	−5	−1	225	25	1	75	15	5
April	55	30	18	10	10	−2	100	100	4	100	−20	−20
May	80	25	14	35	5	−6	1,225	25	36	175	−210	−30
June	20	10	26	−25	−10	6	625	100	36	250	−150	−60
September†	40	20	19	−5	0	−1	25	0	1	0	5	0
October	25	15	27	−20	−5	7	400	25	49	100	−140	−35
November	50	26	23	5	6	3	25	36	9	30	15	18
December	46	19	17	1	−1	−3	1	1	9	−1	−3	3
Total	450	200	200	0	0	0	2,852	314	150	713	−517	−118
Average	45	20	20	0	0	0						

* Deviations from each average are found from the averages for Sales $\bar{S}$, advertising expenditures we incurred $\bar{W}$, and advertising expenditures our competitor incurred $\bar{C}$. For January sales, as an example, $44 - 45 = -1$; for competitive advertising expenditures in June, as another illustration, $26 - 20 = 6$.

† No advertising was done during the slack months of July and August.

ILLUSTRATIVE EXAMPLE

An application of correlation analysis with three variables will highlight the value and procedures of the technique. Management of a certain firm wanted to know the increase in sales volume attributable to various amounts of advertising. Within the locality served by the firm, only one major competitor advertised. It was a relatively simple matter to ascertain his expenditures, since the media rate charges were known. Moreover, since the product involved an installation contract which required official registration, the monthly sales volume of the competitor could be ascertained also. Pertinent data, in abbreviated and simplified form, appear in columns *a, b,* and *c* of Table 7–1, for:

Monthly Sales, in Units, *S;*
Advertising in $100 per Month that we incurred, *W;* and
Advertising in $100 per Month that our competitor incurred, *C.*

It would be difficult to ascertain or estimate the effect of our advertising on sales volume, since obviously the competitive efforts served as a counterweight. Both our advertising expenditures and those of the competitor varied from month to month. A three-dimensional plot of the data (Fig. 7–1, p. 52) does serve to show that there seems to be a joint effect. A large amount of advertising by us leads to higher sales, while at the same time a strong push by the competitor detracts from our efforts. For example, when he spent only $1,400 and we expended $2,500, our sales were high at 80 units. Conversely, when he spent $2,600 and we disbursed a mere $1,000 dollars, our sales dropped to 20 units.

EVALUATING THE EFFECTS

For the purpose of budgeting future advertising, we need relatively precise estimates of its relative effectiveness in the presence of competitive actions. This information is supplied by the estimating equation, as determined by means of the steps in Table 7–2 (p. 53). From this calculation, we observe that:

1. Without any advertising by us or the competitor, we may expect to sell 65 units per month.
2. Advertising by us will bring us further sales of 1.4 units per $100 expended.
3. Competitive advertising will take from us 2.4 units per $100 expended.

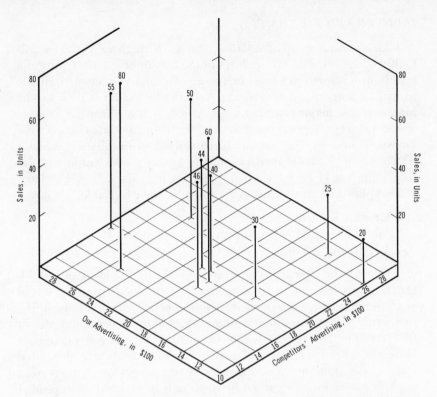

FIGURE 7–1. *Effect of advertising expenditures on sales volume.*

This information could hardly have been obtained without correlation analysis. Management was shocked to learn of the relatively large losses due to the greater effectiveness of the competitor's advertising. A further study was undertaken, which indicated two factors in the competitor's favor:

1. His timing of major promotional expenditures seemed to be better than ours. Thus, even though both firms spent the same total amount of money for advertising, the competitor had discovered the best months for relatively larger or smaller efforts.

2. The competitor's advertising copy was apparently superior to ours.

Management was able to take actions that improved the relative effectiveness of its own efforts while at the same time incurring less of a loss to competitive promotions. Correlation analysis was the catalyst

TABLE 7–2. CALCULATION OF ESTIMATING EQUATION

1. The equation to be found will show the effect of the two advertising variables (W = Advertising We Do; C = Advertising Our Competitor Does) in terms of $100 per month on monthly units sold S. Each variable, W and C, has a constant multiplier, m and n respectively, indicating the rate at which sales change with advertising expenditure. Using the totals of Table 7–1, we obtain:

$$314m - 118n = 713 \text{ (equation 1)}$$
$$-118m + 150n = -517 \text{ (equation 2)}$$

It is easier to discover from the data above what was done than to show the procedure in symbols.

2. Solving equations 1 and 2 for m and n, we obtain:

$$m = 1.38, \text{ or } 1.4 \text{ rounded}$$
$$n = 2.36, \text{ or } 2.4 \text{ rounded}$$

3. Our estimating equation also has a point of origin, found from:

Origin $= 45 - (1.38 \times 20) + (2.36 \times 20) = 64.6$, or 65 rounded (equation 3)

Here the values 45, 20, and 20 represent the averages $\bar{S}$, $\bar{W}$, and, $\bar{C}$, while 1.38 and 2.36 are m and n.

4. Combining these findings, we obtain:

$$S' = 65 + 1.4W - 2.4C \text{ (estimating equation)}$$

S' represents our estimated sales. For example, assume we spend 20 (in $100 per month) on advertising expenditures, while our competitor spends 10, then:

$$\text{Expected Sales } S' = 65 + (1.4 \times 20) - (2.4 \times 10) = 69 \text{ units}$$

5. As a general conclusion, note that (1) In the absence of competitive advertising, we may expect to sell 65 units plus 1.4 additional units per $100 of our advertising. (2) Any $100 that our competitor spends on advertising will take 2.4 units away from us.

that brought about the sequence of studies and actions leading to the firm's improved position in the marketplace.

LARGE-SCALE APPLICATION OF CORRELATION ANALYSIS

What has been presented is a simplified version of the real-life situation, which included the following additional facets:

1. Data for 3 years were studied.
2. A statistical method was used to remove all effects of seasonal fluctuation (even though these were small).

Making a Correlation Analysis   *53*

3. Advertising costs were broken down by type (newspaper and radio).

4. An allowance for lag was incorporated, representing the average interval (though short) between occurrence of the advertising and response from customers.

With further statistical methods, the validity of the correlation was checked. The multiple correlation coefficient was found to be 0.84 or "good." Normally, scale values are interpreted as follows: 0.9 = very good, 0.8 = good, 0.7 = fair, 0.6 = borderline, and anything below 0.6 = relatively poor. The coefficient cannot be above 1.0. A further measure of the precision of the estimates was determined by calculating the *standard error of estimate,* which was found to represent 9.6, or roughly 10 units. This is slightly greater than 20 per cent of the average 45 units sold per month. A statistical interpretation of this value is that odds are 2 to 1 that a predicted effect of advertising effort will be correct within ± 20 per cent.

The calculation of the estimating equation, correlation coefficient, and error term for a multiple correlation coefficient involving many variables is, today, a matter of minutes on a computer. Performing this task manually or with a desk calculator is of value for purposes of understanding the method (as was done in our example).

FURTHER USES OF CORRELATION ANALYSIS

Here are a few more of a multitude of instances in which correlation analysis is of service to marketing and sales:

1. One firm correlated its sales to several key economic-indicator time series. The published forecasts for these nationwide data could then be multiplied by suitable factors to show the expected sales volume for the firm. Upon review and revision where needed, the final forecasts obtained served in planning promotions, production schedules, and inventory buildups.

2. An office-equipment manufacturer was able to establish realistic sales quotas for each of his 12 territories by correlating expected sales with various pertinent data on (1) the number of plants and offices in each area, (2) the total sales of all office-equipment manufacturers, and (3) the number of business telephones in each territory. Subsequently, a further refinement in the quotas was attained by the addition of 5 more data series related to the need for office equipment.

3. A candy-bar manufacturer had been using a variety of promotional media—magazines, radio, and television. The amount of each of these types of advertising varied for different time periods. By means of a multiple correlation analysis, the relative contribution of each type of advertisement to total sales was established. Next, cost-effectiveness ratios were set up, comparing the expenditures against the revenue gained. Revisions in the program were made, leading to larger sales volume without increasing the total advertising budget.

There are thus many types of correlation analyses that can be of value to a business organization.

THE AVERAGE RELATIONSHIP

The discussion has been in terms of multiple correlation, since usually there are a number of factors that must be considered in their effect on over-all results. Thus, if the volume of sales is considered the over-all result, or "output variable" (also known as the "dependent variable"), we will usually be able to point to a number of "input variables" (or "independent variables") that jointly produce the result observed. Nevertheless, occasions arise when there are only two variables: one, dependent; and the other, independent.

A typical instance of such an application occurs when a firm wishes to correlate its own performance against an industrywide index. Usually, extensive and elaborate market analyses and research efforts, expended by a trade association or by the government, will result in a relatively sophisticated forecast of industry, trade-area, or other business expectations for the coming year. Often, several groups may make forecasts, from which a single forecast can be prepared by weighting and averaging the individual estimates. The question to be answered for an individual firm is then: How well are our own business-volume data correlated with the general forecast?

In order to provide an answer to this question, a simple correlation analysis may be performed for the following:

1. A general forecast for the past years (such as an index prepared by trade associations, government agencies, or others, utilizing suitable averaging when several data sets are available). This general forecast is considered the "independent variable."

2. The individual firm's own business experience in the corresponding years (such as sales volume). This type of data is considered

TABLE 7–3. RELATION OF INDUSTRY ACTIVITY TO FIRM'S SALES

Year	Firm's Annual Sales Volume, $100,000, S	Index of Industry Activity I	Deviations from Average*		Squared Deviations†		Cross-Product‡
			$S - \overline{S}$ $= s$	$I - \overline{I}$ $= i$	s^2	i^2	$s \times i$
1963	26	50	−24	−50	576	2,500	1,200
1964	50	70	0	−30	0	900	0
1965	40	94	−10	−6	100	36	60
1966	60	140	+10	+40	100	1,600	400
1967	54	104	+4	+4	16	16	16
1968	70	142	+20	+42	400	1,764	840
Total	300	600	0	0	1,192	6,816	2,516
Average	50	100			—	—	—

* Averages are $\overline{S} = 50$ and $\overline{I} = 100$. The deviations $S - \overline{S}$ and $I - \overline{I}$ are denoted by small s and i.

† To find squared deviations, we multiply individual deviations. For example, for $s = -24$, $s^2 = (-24)^2 = 576$.

‡ The cross-product represents the multiplication of $s \times i$. In the first row, $(-24) \times (50) = 1,200$.

Note that the firm's sales S are considered at least in large part a function of the industry activity I. Therefore, S is considered dependent on I. In other words, S is the dependent variable, and I the independent variable.

In order to evaluate the degree of relationship existing, a correlation coefficient may be determined, utilizing the data computed above. The procedure is easier to follow in terms of the actual figures than to utilize symbols. We obtain:

Correlation Coefficient $r = 2516 \div \sqrt{1192 \times 6816} = 0.88$ rounded, thus signifying from good to very-good correlation.

the "dependent variable," thereby viewing the individual firm's results as being influenced by general business conditions in the industry. (In turn, industry conditions may be a function of general economic factors, nationwide and worldwide, but we will not be concerned with those here. Separate analyses of these effects, again utilizing correlation techniques, can, of course, be made.)

If the correlation analysis performed reveals a relatively close relationship between the firm's past business experience and the general forecast, then the *average relationship* found can be utilized for future forecasts of the firm's expectations. The average relationship will be expressed in terms of a regression line. Let us look at some specific figures, such as those given in Table 7–3, showing a company's annual sales volume (dependent variable) and a general index of business ac-

Step	Calculation					
1	Use averages and totals from prior calculations.					

Total Number	Averages		Totals or Sums (Σ)		
of Years, N	$\bar{S}$	$\bar{I}$	Σs^2	Σi^2	Σsi
6	50	100	1,192	6,816	2,536

Step	Calculation
2	Find slope b of forecasting equation. Note that this equation relates firm's sales S to industry activity I. $$b = (\Sigma si)/(\Sigma i^2) = 2,516/6,816 = 0.4 \text{ rounded}$$
3	Find origin a of forecasting equation. $$a = \bar{S} - b\bar{I} = 50 - 0.4(100) = 10$$
4	Combine slope and origin to obtain forecasting equation for forecast values $S.'$ $$S' = a + bI = 10 + 0.4I$$
5	Use the forecasting equation. For example, if industry activity I is anticipated at an index of 160 next year, then: $$S' = 10 + 0.4(160) = 10 + 64 = 74$$
6	Make the forecast. From an anticipated sales volume of 74 (in \$100,000) from step 5, the firm's forecast for next year is \$7.4 million.

tivity for the industry (independent variable). Supplementary Table 7–4 leads to the calculation of the regression equation:

$$S' = 10 + 0.4 \times I$$

Here S' is the forecast for the firm's sales volume for the coming year, based on an analysis of past correlations; I represents the forecast made by a generalized industry index. For example, assuming that the index is predicted to reach 160 next year, we obtain the following forecast for the company:

$$S' = 10 + 0.4 \times 160 = 74$$

Since sales are stated in \$100,000, multiplying 74 by this monetary figure yields \$7,400,000 as the forecast for the company's sales during the coming year. The results are plotted in Figure 7–2 (p. 58).

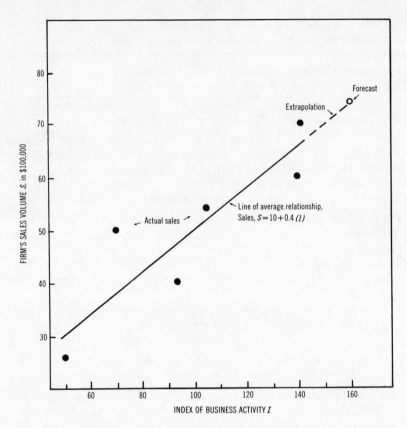

FIGURE 7–2. *Industry activity related to firm's sales.* From the past average relationship of business activity in the industry, as measured by an index *I* and the firm's sales experience *S*, a close enough relationship is noted to permit a projection of future expectations. For this example, the following comparison can be noted:

							Total
Sales Volume, in $100,000	26	50	40	60	54	70	300
Index of Business Activity	50	70	94	140	104	142	600

MEASURING THE AMOUNT OF CORRELATION

The reliability that can be placed in a regression equation depends on two factors: (1) the extent to which past trends and relationships may be expected to hold in the future, and (2) the amount of correlation present in the data. The first factor is subject primarily to personal judgment and experience, while the second can be evaluated in quantitative terms, utilizing the correlation coefficient. Calculations leading to this value are shown in the lower section of Table 7–3.

Once the correlation coefficient has been calculated, the questions to be answered are: (1) How good is the relationship shown? (2) How significant is it? As noted earlier, a coefficient within a range of 0.6 to 1.0 denotes from "fair" to "good" correlation. In fact, an actual value of 1.0 should never be expected in practice, because various factors would prevent a "perfect" correlation as implied by this coefficient. It is, however, possible that an observed correlation may be the result of chance configuration of data points. Mere chance is particularly important as a possibility when only a few data points are used. Thus, in addition to being from "fair" to "good," it is also desirable for a correlation to be "significant." This means we should establish, at some level of confidence (usually 90 or 95 per cent), that no chance configuration exists.

For our illustrative example of the relationship of industry activity to an individual firm's sales, we correlated 6 sets of points. Now, any 2 points on a graph will always form a line and thus give a seemingly "perfect" correlation. In fact, such a "correlation" is meaningless. For 6 points, we have $6 - 2 = 4$ points beyond the level of meaninglessness. This 4 is called *degrees of freedom*. Entering Table 7–5 (p. 60) at this level, we find that a minimal value of 0.73 and 0.81 is required for the correlation coefficient at confidence levels of 90 and 95 per cent respectively. The actual correlation coefficient found for our example is well above that, at 0.89. It is thus significant.

CAUTIONS IN USING CORRELATION ANALYSIS

Computational techniques that establish a certain degree of correlation are, in fact, merely methods to define an association between two or more variables. Association, in turn, does not necessarily imply causation. Accordingly, the mechanically developed findings from correlation and regression equations and plottings must be evaluated carefully by management and staff people alike. As with all quantitative tools, the techniques discussed in this chapter are thus subject to verification, assessment, judgment, and evaluation on the basis of qualitative factors before final conclusions can be reached and decisions made.

TABLE 7-5. MINIMUM VALUES OF CORRELATION COEFFICIENT
r NEEDED TO ESTABLISH SIGNIFICANCE

Degrees of Freedom*	Confidence Level, Per Cent, at Which Significance of Correlation Is to Be Established	
	90	95
1	0.99	0.99
2	0.90	0.95
3	0.81	0.88
4	0.73	0.81
5	0.67	0.75
6	0.62	0.71
8	0.55	0.63
10	0.50	0.58
15	0.41	0.48
20	0.36	0.42
25	0.32	0.38
30	0.30	0.35
40	0.26	0.30
50	0.23	0.27
60	0.21	0.25
80	0.18	0.22
100	0.16	0.20

* Degrees of freedom represent the number n of sets of data minus the number k of variables in the correlation. For the text example of business activity versus sales volume, there were 6 sets of data (yielding 6 points on the scatter diagram of Figure 7-2). There were 2 variables. Thus $n - k = 6 - 2 = 4 =$ degrees of freedom.

Generally, it is not enough for a correlation to be fair or better; it should also be significant. However, when the degrees of freedom are large, it is possible for a poor correlation to be "significant," as the lower portions of the tabular values show. Such significance means that there is probably a nonchance relationship among the variables investigated, but the correlation is "poor" because other as yet unidentified variables have not been included in the analysis.

SOURCE: "Percentage Points for the Distribution of the Correlation Coefficient," with adaptations, from E. S. Pearson and H. O. Hartley, eds., *Biometrika Tables for Statisticians* (New York: Cambridge University Press, 1958), Vol. I.

SUMMARY

When the effect of one or more factors must be evaluated in relation to expected sales volume, correlation analysis is a highly useful tool. Based on the information obtained, intelligent plans can be developed for effective future promotional programs, merchandising, marketing, production, and inventory buildup.

Correlations can be made at several levels. For example, various factors within the firm can be related to sales volume. Alternatively, the analysis can be extended to include competitive factors and industry forecasts. Finally, sales of the individual firm can also be correlated with the economy as a whole and with the forecasts for the economy. Before the results of a correlation analysis are applied, we should assure ourselves that the correlation is valid, in terms of the actual coefficient obtained and its significance as well as in terms of qualitative evaluations.

CHAPTER 8

Predicting Market Share

What share of the market to expect for the immediate future and the more distant future is a weighty issue for any producer faced with accelerating advances in technology and product innovation, together with more diversified distribution channels and a sharpening of domestic and foreign competition. But while market-share anticipations are crucial for both the producer and the consumer-goods industries, manufacturers in the latter category face special evaluation and anticipation problems because of the multitude of customers to be satisfied.

We are all familiar with those advertising slogans whose objective is to win customers from other brands while holding on to current consumers: "I'd rather fight than switch"; "When I changed to _____, I changed for good"; "Come on over to _____." These reflect not only a widespread marketing concern but also a problem of great managerial importance: to assess a firm's present market position, and to predict its future position, in terms of consumer-patronage decisions.

THE MARKOV CHAIN PROCESS

For the purpose of evaluating market shares that are to be anticipated for the future, the Markov Chain Process is a powerful technique. Originated early in this century as a means of analyzing the current movement of a set of variables to predict their future movement, so as to gain a better comprehension of various phenomena in the physical sciences, this method has more recently been adapted for marketing needs.

The Markov Chain Process serves to illuminate the ultimate effects of various market trends, providing useful conclusions regarding key consumer tendencies in relation to a firm's present and future market position. The principal types of information derived from Markov analysis are:

1. Present and future market shares to be anticipated.
2. Rates at which future market shares are being won or lost.

3. The nature of prevailing trends, such as the market equilibrium (if any) toward which current developments may tend to lead.

4. Evaluation of the results of current and planned promotional campaigns in relation to market gains.

One of the ironies of the Markov Chain Process is that the market shares it predicts will usually hold true only for the relatively near future. The reason is that long-range forecasts invariably spur management to take immediate strong measures to forestall anticipated losses or secure bigger gains, and these counterattacks inevitably reshape the picture.

In many industries, therefore, exchange of customers among various competing brands is a result of two prime factors:

1. Consumers generally switch brands not at random, but in some relatively stable pattern. These consumer choices, in turn, are reflected in the propensities of various brands to retain, lose, and attract patronage in the marketplace.

2. Realizing the effects of consumer choice on current and future market-share expectations, alert competing firms take various countermeasures.

Although consumer tendencies can be recognized without a formal Markov Chain Process, as a matter of simple judgment, a more scientific approach, evaluating the expected effects of various market movements by a Markov analysis, will have a decided advantage. It will provide management with precise data on the direction in which current consumer and market tendencies are leading. Suitable market strategies can then be planned, and adequate financing provided for them, in a highly informed manner. The result is a better allocation of the firm's marketing resources in terms of promotion, distribution, manpower, and finances.

CONSUMER BEHAVIOR PATTERN

Sample-survey data provide the essential information regarding consumer behavior patterns on which the Markov analysis is built. In recent years, the number of such surveys and of firms providing them has grown. A favored device is the randomly selected group of sample families—the "consumer panel"—who record their purchases of brand-name goods. The proportion of consumers who stay with a brand and the proportion who change from one brand to another, as

BRAND BOUGHT IN INITIAL PERIOD	PERCENTAGE OF CONSUMERS REMAINING LOYAL OR SWITCHING DURING SECOND PERIOD		
	A	B	C
A	60 loyal	10 $A \rightarrow B$	30 $A \rightarrow C$
B	0 $B \rightarrow A$	80 loyal	20 $B \rightarrow C$
C	40 $C \rightarrow A$	0 $C \rightarrow B$	60 loyal

FIGURE 8–1. *Consumer behavior pattern in regard to brand loyalty and brand switching.* The arrows indicate the direction of switch, from brand in initial period to brand in second period. Thus 60 per cent of the customers remained loyal to *A,* but 10 per cent switched from *A* to *B* and 30 per cent moved from *A* to *C.*

revealed in the sample, are then taken as an approximate measure of the percentages prevailing nationwide or within the area under study.

The diagram in Figure 8–1 illustrates in simplified form (using only 3 brands instead of a more realistic 30 items) the information provided by a sample survey. Observe that the following percentages of users remained loyal to their respective brands *A, B,* and *C:* 60, 80, and 60 per cent. Others, however, changed brands. Of those who had initially purchased *A,* 10 per cent changed to *B* in the transition from the first period to the end of the second period. Another 30 per cent switched from *A* to *C.* Of the initial *B* customers, none moved to *A,* 80 per cent stayed with *B,* and 20 per cent switched to *C.* For *C,* we find that 40 per cent moved to *A,* none to *B,* and 60 per cent remained loyal. For each row, the total adds up to the expected 100 per cent.

PREDICTING MARKET SHARE IN THE SECOND PERIOD

If the patterns diagramed in Figure 8–1 can be expected to prevail for the next market period, then it will be possible to predict the changes that will occur in relative market shares among the competing brands. Assume, for example, that the 3 brands enjoyed these shares of the total initial buying period:

Brand	Market Share
A	30%
B	20%
C	50%

Under the impact of consumer actions during the coming period, these shares must be expected to change. A simple set of calculations, provided by the Markov Chain Process, reveals that the market shares will change, for brands *A, B,* and *C,* to 38, 19, and 43 per cent. As previously, the total of the market shares remains 100 per cent, but the division of the market has shifted in favor of *A* and to the detriment of *B* and *C.* The calculations leading to these results may be studied in Table 8–1 (p. 66).

The assumption that the consumer's past pattern will not change unduly is inherent in the calculation process. Such a notion may be hard for the "practical expert" to accept, because in a dynamic marketing situation we do observe effects of various special factors—the promotional campaigns initiated by competitive groups.

Let the skeptic, however, consider the following factors:

1. Even though various competitive actions may alter the original predictions, it is nevertheless desirable to know the chain of events that would tend to prevail in the absence of special promotional efforts by the individual firm or its competitors.

2. In the course of time, as the initial effects of various competitive actions become known, proper modifications may be incorporated in the Markov Chain Process to allow for these influences.

3. Only by means of a Markov analysis can the precise promotional needs of a firm be determined, so as to relate manpower and monetary expenditures to foreseeable benefits, and to compare actual results with expected accomplishments.

TABLE 8–1. EVALUATION OF MARKET SHARE IN SECOND PERIOD

a	b	c*	d*	e*	f	g	h	i	j	k†	l‡
		Anticipations for Second Period				Effect of Consumer Behavior Pattern on Market Share					
		Percentage of Consumers Remaining Loyal or Switching				$b \times c$	$b \times d$	$b \times e$			
	Market Share in Initial Period, Per Cent	A	B	C	Total	A	B	C	Check Total	New Market Share, Per Cent	Gain (+) or Loss (−), Per Cent
Brand											
A	30	60	10	30	100	18	3	9	30	38	+8
B	20	0	80	20	100	0	16	4	20	19	−1
C	50	40	0	60	100	20	0	30	50	43	−7
Total	100	100	90	110	300	38	19	43	100	100	0

* In columns c, d, and e, some consumers remain loyal. For example, 60 per cent of those who bought brand A in the initial period buy A in the second period; but 10 per cent of those who bought A initially buy B in the second period and 30 per cent buy C. A zero indicates that no switching has occurred, such as from B to A. Only the diagonal figures (60, 80, and 60 in this example) show brand loyalties; the remainder show switching (including 0 percentages switched).

† New market share k is the total for A, B, and C under columns g, h, and i.

‡ From column l, we observe that brand A has gained 8 per cent (from $k - b$), but brands B and C have lost ($19 - 20 = -1$ and $43 - 50 = -7$).

66

As with all techniques of executive analysis, planning, decision making, and control, the Markov Chain Process is no substitute for executive judgment. It merely serves to quantify and evaluate in relative and measurable dimensions the basic inputs developed as a result of cooperation between the executive and his management-science specialists. We can thus readily agree with the skeptic that Markov analysis is not a method of marketing, but merely an aid to planning and decision making in effective, economical, and goal-conscious modern marketing. Moreover, the growing number of firms who rely on this quantitative approach testify to its usefulness in the context of actual marketing problems.

If market-share anticipations are to be fully valuable, they must be evaluated for several periods. Moreover, an indication must be provided as to the final equilibrium position to be expected under prevailing conditions and consumer tendencies. The need for such predictions of the future is readily apparent: promotional expenditures are made not only for the immediate future but also for the long range. The manner in which the Markov Chain Process is extended toward further market periods will be discussed in Chapter 9.

SUMMARY

The Markov Chain Process is a technique which is being used increasingly by consumer-goods manufacturers to assess a company's present market position and to predict its future position, in terms of the consumer's propensity to switch brands. Based on the assumption that the brand-switching pattern is stable and therefore measurable, rather than random, Markov analysis can provide management with precise data on the direction in which current consumer and market tendencies are leading.

CHAPTER 9

Predicting Market Share
for Several Periods

A typical case history will serve to demonstrate the vital need for market-share predictions. Impressed by the large sales volume for a new
product, a manufacturer rushed to complete an expensive enlargement
of processing facilities—only to have this equipment stay idle. What
had happened? A quick survey revealed that people had bought his
product readily, but only once. With brand loyalty poor, it was not
possible to achieve a sustained volume of sales once the supply of potential new purchasers had been exhausted.

One among hundreds that could be cited, this experience emphasizes the fact that simple sales figures and data on market shares are not
enough for responsible decision making. We must also know what proportion of people will return to buy our product a second, third, or
fourth time, to be sure that we are not just riding the crest of a fad.
Moreover, it will be desirable to have breakdowns of data on consumer
purchasing by types of buyers and marketing channels or outlets. Distribution plans and future promotional efforts can then be guided accordingly.

EXTENDING THE MARKOV CHAIN

We have seen how initial market share, combined with customers'
revealed tendencies toward brand loyalty or switching, can be used to
predict the market share in the second period. The diagram used for
this purpose, as developed in Chapter 8 (Figure 8–1), can now be employed to extend our predictions to the third, fourth, and subsequent
periods. Let us study, for example, what proportion of consumers will
have remained loyal to brand A by the end of the third period. Note
the following:

1. From period 1 to period 2, 60 per cent of the consumers re-

mained loyal to A. If this pattern continues for the transition from period 2 to period 3, then at the end of period 3 the percentage of people who bought A in period 1 and again in period 3 will be 60 per cent × 60 per cent, giving a net remaining loyalty of 36 per cent.

2. During the transition to period 3, we might normally expect to regain some of the customers (10 per cent in our example) who moved from A to B in period 2. In the present instance, however, we note from the intersection of row B and column A that no such return movement occurred (the entry is 0 per cent).

3. During period 3 we will regain some customers for A who had been lost to C in period 2. In particular, 30 per cent had been lost (intersection of row A and column C), of whom 40 per cent will now go back to A (intersection of row C and column A). The net regain is thus 40 per cent × 30 per cent, giving 12 per cent as the result.

4. Finally, adding up the percentage values of 36, 0, and 12 gives a total of 48 per cent of the consumers who bought brand A in period 1 and will do so in period 3. Other loyalties and switches among brands are evaluated similarly. Table 9–1 (p. 70) provides a convenient summary of the calculations.

The totals for consumer-patronage tendencies relating to period 3 are utilized in columns c, d, and e of Table 9–2 (p. 71), which yields the anticipated market shares for period 3. The calculations are parallel to those previously shown for period 2.

Further extensions to periods 4 and 5 are provided in Tables 9–3 (p. 72) and 9–4 (p. 73).

USING THE RESULTS

With the mathematical procedures completed, we must now consider their significance for management. Assume that ours is brand A. The trend shows that our market share will have advanced to 40 per cent by the end of period 5, compared to an initial 30 per cent. This is certainly comforting. Our gain, however, will be coming primarily from losses incurred by brand C, which is currently strongest, with 50 per cent of the market. Surely, C's management will take countermeasures. This competitor must be watched closely, and we will certainly try to prevent a reversal of current favorable trends.

A hint in the direction of desirable policies is given by the diagram itself. Note that C and we enjoy the same customer loyalties, but

[to page 74]

TABLE 9–1. ANTICIPATED EFFECTS OF BRAND LOYALTY AND BRAND SWITCHING ON MARKET SHARE IN THIRD PERIOD

| Brand Bought in Initial Period | Percentage of Customers Who Initially Bought Brand to the Left and Who May Be Expected to Buy Brand Shown Below in Third Period | | | |
	A	B	C	Total
A	60 × 60 = 36.00 10 × 0 = 0 30 × 40 = 12.00	60 × 10 = 6.00 10 × 80 = 8.00 30 × 0 = 0	60 × 30 = 18.00 10 × 20 = 2.00 30 × 60 = 18.00	
	Total 48.00	Total 14.00	Total 38.00	100
B	0 × 60 = 0 80 × 0 = 0 20 × 40 = 8.00	0 × 10 = 0 80 × 80 = 64.00 20 × 0 = 0	0 × 30 = 0 80 × 20 = 16.00 20 × 60 = 12.00	
	Total 8.00	Total 64.00	Total 28.00	100
C	40 × 60 = 24.00 0 × 0 = 0 60 × 40 = 24.00	40 × 10 = 4.00 0 × 80 = 0 60 × 0 = 0	40 × 30 = 12.00 0 × 20 = 0 60 × 60 = 36.00	
	Total 48.00	Total 4.00	Total 48.00	100

EXPLANATION

The calculations will be explained using the cell in the upper left-hand corner as an illustration.

1. Since 60 per cent of the consumers remained loyal to brand A from period 1 to period 2, a continuing similar pattern should leave $0.60 \times 0.60 = 0.36$, or 36 per cent who will have remained loyal from period 1 through period 3.

2. In period 3, brand A may usually hope to regain some customers (10 per cent in our example, as Figure 8–1 shows) who moved from A to B in period 2. In this instance, however, the zero in row B and column A of that figure indicates that no such return movement has occurred.

3. Some consumers for A, who had been lost to C in period 2, will move back to A in period 3. Of the 30 per cent lost (row A, column C intersection of Figure 8–1), 40 per cent will now move back to A (row C, column A intersection). The net regain is thus 0.30×0.40, or 12 per cent.

4. Finally, adding the 3 percentages found gives a total of 48 per cent of consumers who bought brand A in period 1 and may be expected to do so again in period 3.

Table 9–2. Evaluation of Market Share in Third Period

a	b	c*	d*	e*	f*	g	h	i	j	k	l	m†
						Anticipations for Third Period						
		Percentage of Consumers Remaining Loyal or Switching				*Effect of Consumer Behavior Pattern on Market Share*					*Gain (+) or Loss (−), Per Cent*	
	Market Share in Initial Period, Per Cent					$b \times c$	$b \times d$	$b \times e$	*Check Total*	*New Market Share, Per Cent*	*Third Period vs. Initial Period*	*Third Period vs. Second Period*
Brand		A	B	C	*Total*	A	B	C				
A	30	48	14	38	100	14.4	4.2	11.4	30	40	+10	+2
B	20	8	64	28	100	1.6	12.8	5.6	20	19	−1	0
C	50	48	4	48	100	24.0	2.0	24.0	50	41	−9	−2
Total	100	104	82	114	300	40.0	19.0	41.0	100	100	0	0

* Calculations proceed as for Table 8–1, except that the new entries for columns c, d, e, and f come from the determinations in Table 9–1.

† For comparison in column m, refer to column k in Table 8–1. Observe that although the amount of change in market shares (column l) has increased for the third period, the increase has occurred at a slower rate (comparison in column m), indicating that we are approaching an equilibrium condition for market-share distribution.

TABLE 9–3. EVALUATION OF MARKET SHARE IN FOURTH PERIOD

a	b	c	d	e	f	g	h	i	j	k	l	m*
											Gain (+) or Loss (−), Per Cent	
											Fourth Period vs. Initial Period	Fourth Period vs. Third Period
										New Market Share, Per Cent		
									Check Total			
			Anticipations for Fourth Period			Effect of Consumer Behavior Pattern on Market Share						
						b × c	*b × d*	*b × e*				
	Market Share in Initial Period, Per Cent	Percentage of Consumers Remaining Loyal or Switching				*A*	*B*	*C*				
Brand		*A*	*B*	*C*	Total							
A	30	42.4	17.2	40.4	100	12.72	5.16	12.12	30	40.4	+10.4	+0.4
B	20	22.4	43.2	34.4	100	4.48	8.64	6.88	20	19.4	−0.6	+0.4
C	50	46.4	11.2	42.4	100	23.20	5.60	21.20	50	40.2	−9.8	−0.8
Total	100	111.2	71.6	117.2	300	40.40	19.40	40.20	100	100.0	0	0

* This fourth period is showing markedly less change in column m than in l. We are rapidly approaching the equilibrium state. It can be shown that at equilibrium the market shares for brands A, B, and C will be 40, 20, and 40 per cent.

TABLE 9–4. EVALUATION OF MARKET SHARE IN FIFTH PERIOD

a	b	c	d	e	f	g	h	i	j	k*	l	m
						Anticipations for Fifth Period					Gain (+) or Loss (−), Per Cent	
							Effect of Consumer Behavior Pattern on Market Share				Fifth Period vs. Initial Period	Fifth Period vs. Fourth Period
	Market Share in Initial Period, Per Cent	Percentage of Consumers Remaining Loyal or Switching				$b \times c$	$b \times d$	$b \times e$	Check Total	New Market Share, Per Cent		
Brand		A	B	C	Total	A	B	C				
A	30	40.576	19.248	40.176	100	12.1728	5.7744	12.0528	30	40.128	+10.128	−0.272
B	20	35.136	26.368	38.496	100	7.0272	5.2736	7.6992	20	19.832	−0.168	+0.432
C	50	41.856	17.568	40.576	100	20.9280	8.7840	20.2880	50	40.040	−9.960	−0.160
Total	100	117.568	63.184	119.248	300	40.1280	19.8320	40.0400	100	100.000	0	0

* For this fifth period, the market shares have reached a position near the ultimate "steady-state" equilibrium condition. In fact, rounding the percentages in column k yields 40, 20, and 40 per cent, which in turn are the steady-state values.

73

[*from page 69*]

while we lose 30 per cent of our customers to him, he in turn loses 40 per cent to us. *C*'s likely move will thus be to seek to retain more of his customers, either through special promotional endeavors or by providing better service. For us, too, efforts to retain more of the current customers would seem desirable.

The final plans and policies evolved will depend on a review of dynamic marketing factors, together with various brand differences such as design, packaging, outlets, types of buyers, distribution channels, and regional differences. Compilation of all pertinent data will permit making the cost and effectiveness analyses essential for further promotional plans and for justifying the expenditures they entail.

The Markov Chain Process is thus an aid to marketing in terms of more informed, precisely quantified decision making.

SUMMARY

The effect on a company's market share of the interplay among competing brands, resulting from consumer buying decisions, has been demonstrated. It is not enough, however, merely to predict such effects from one selling period to the next. Forecasts must extend over several buying cycles, so that both long-range and short-range planning can be geared to anticipations.

CHAPTER 10

Predicting Market Share during the Equilibrium Period

Disruption of market equilibrium must be expected whenever a new brand is introduced. Extensive "get-acquainted" discounts, premium coupons, and other special advertising efforts usually accompany the entrance of the new product, and the repercussions will be felt throughout the market.

Such costly promotions cannot continue indefinitely, however, and their prime justification is to gain a foothold for the new brand. Thereafter, a new relative relationship will exist among the competing brands, all of which will be subject to the continuing interplay of brand loyalties and switches that reflect consumer-patronage tendencies.

EQUILIBRIUM MARKET SHARE

When the repercussions and adjustments in the market resulting from the introduction of a new brand have worked themselves out, a new set of strengths will have developed among the brands and their hold on market shares and consumer loyalties. The old equilibrium has been replaced, and a new set of forces has been set into motion. The important question to be answered next is: What will be the ultimate market share that may be anticipated under the new grouping of brands? An example will illustrate.

Assume that a new brand *A* has been introduced in the market and that the initial period of major adjustments has ended. Relative stability exists, but consumers will be doing further switching, as revealed in the diagram of Figure 8–1, introduced in Chapter 8, but also applicable now.

Brand *A* has achieved a market share of 30 per cent, leaving 20 per cent to *B* and 50 per cent to *C*. Using these figures and the diagram, we can anticipate the shares of the next period and we can also make predictions regarding several subsequent periods, as shown in Chapters 8 and 9. But we can also go a step further, and in effect calculate the ultimate market shares that must be expected unless counteractions are taken. This condition represents that state of the market, in terms of market shares, that will prevail after a sufficient number of successive buying periods has elapsed for the market to come to a new stable state—the equilibrium.

EVALUATING THE EQUILIBRIUM STATE

Using the illustrative data given above, we can evaluate the expected equilibrium state by means of the steps given in Table 10–1. From this calculation, the following is observed:

| | Market Shares, Per Cent | |
| | Initial (Current) | Equilibrium State |
Brand	State	Expected
A	30	40
B	20	20
C	50	40

The additional gain of 10 per cent for *A* will be at the expense of *C*. How soon and how effectively the management of brand *C* will take countermeasures will depend to a large extent on its alertness in watching the market and in assessing trends—such as by means of the Markov Chain Process. In a real-life situation, where a large number of competing brands vie for the consumer's patronage, there may be a great deal of action, counteraction, and reaction among suppliers. The analysis then becomes more complex than in a simple 3-brand case, but it becomes even more essential for the firm intent on maintaining or increasing its market share.

DECISION MAKING BASED ON MARKET DATA

Facts are the basis of sound management decisions, and the Markov Chain Process provides a crucial link by indicating consumer tendencies either to stay loyal or to switch and by predicting the market

TABLE 10–1. EVALUATION OF MARKET SHARE IN EQUILIBRIUM STATE

Step	Calculation
1	Denote the equilibrium-state market shares, in decimal fraction form, by A, B, and C for the 3 brands A, B, and C. Observe the original fractions as dependent on loyalties and switches, revealed in the original transition diagram (Figure 8–1). For A, for example, 0.6 of the consumers remained loyal, none switched from B to A, but 0.4 switched from C to A. For B, 0.1 will switch from A, 0.8 will remain loyal, and none will be gained from C. For C, the fractions are 0.3, 0.2, and 0.6 for gains from A and B and loyalty to C.

| 2 | Express the relations just observed in equations 1, 2, and 3 below; observe that all market-share fractions must add up to 1.0, or 100 per cent. |

$$0.6A + \quad 0 \quad + 0.4C = A \quad \text{or} \quad -0.4A + \quad 0 \quad + 0.4C = 0 \quad \text{(equation 1)}$$
$$0.1A + 0.8B + \quad 0 \quad = B \quad \text{or} \quad 0.1A - 0.2B + \quad 0 \quad = 0 \quad \text{(equation 2)}$$
$$0.3A + 0.2B + 0.6C = C \quad \text{or} \quad 0.3A + 0.2B - 0.4C = 0 \quad \text{(equation 3)}$$
$$A + \quad B + \quad C = 1.0 \quad\quad\quad\quad\quad\quad\quad\quad\quad\quad\quad\quad\quad \text{(equation 4)}$$

| 3 | First add equations 1 + 3 and then 2 + 3, as shown to the right above, giving: |

$$-0.1A + 0.2B + 0 = 0$$
$$0.4A + 0 - 0.4C = 0$$

Therefore, $0.2B = 0.1A$, so that $B = 0.5A$ and $A = 2B$. Also, $0.4A = 0.4C$ and $A = C$.

Substituting $B = 0.5A$ in equation 4 shows that $A + 0.5A + C = 1$ or $1.5A + C = 1$. But since $C = A$, $1.5A + A = 1$ means that $2.5A = 1$, and therefore A must be 0.4. C is also 0.4, because $C = A$. Moreover, since $A = 2B$, B must be 0.2.

| 4 | Having found the equilibrium-condition market shares of 0.4, 0.2, and 0.4 for brands A, B, and C, we conclude that the ultimate state of the market (unless disturbed by new factors) will lead to the following: |

Market	Brand		
Share	A	B	C
Decimal	0.4	0.2	0.4
Per Cent	40.0	20.0	40.0

shares to be expected in the next stage, in subsequent stages, and in the ultimate equilibrium stage. Recognizing the trends and where they are pointing, management is in a good position to allocate funds in support of programs designed to accomplish feasible objectives, actions, and counteractions. Production as well as promotional goals can be shaped accordingly. Here are some of the questions that can be answered by proper analysis:

1. How effective are various types of promotional efforts? Data

will come from a review of copy, media, locality, and other factors in past promotions and their effects on consumer-patronage decisions.

2. How important are service and quality? Answers will be developed from a consideration of the effects of service and product quality on consumer loyalty.

3. Should productive capacity be expanded? The Markov Chain Process will yield important clues as to whether or not future market demand will warrant plant and equipment expansion.

Decision making based on the forecasting methods discussed here is far from being risk-free. Uncertainty and unforeseeable events will continue to pose weighty problems whenever long-term decisions must be made. However, analysis of the market in terms of Markov chains will serve management by providing a better insight into the interplay of market forces and by giving early indications of developing trends and tendencies in the market.

SUMMARY

The Markov Chain Process gives market insights that are superior to mere comparison of "before" and "after" results of various types of advertising, distribution methods, service policies, or product qualities. The analysis goes beyond the immediate effects of such factors by measuring the long-term impact on successive and ultimate market stages. The true merits of various potential courses of action can thus be evaluated realistically with both the short-term and the long-term anticipation in mind. Decision making based on such information is likely to yield the greatest returns.

CHAPTER 11

Coping with Market Uncertainties

Uncertainties regarding economic and marketing conditions, manpower availabilities, and costs are among the many factors that have a significant bearing on such sales and marketing questions as:

1. What prices will we be able to charge?
2. What profit will that leave us?
3. Will there be a good market for our new product?
4. What is our competition coming out with?

These considerations involve many factors that cannot be predicted with assurance, but we can nevertheless seek to develop forecasts to the best of our abilities, utilizing all available pertinent information. In recent years, moreover, powerful new approaches have been developed. These permit the sales and marketing planner to cope effectively with the factors of uncertainty and to arrive at over-all strategies that take cognizance of contingencies. In this chapter, we will examine the logic and procedures involved in one new approach, which has been finding increasing favor among responsible executives harassed by the problem of decision making under highly variable economic, technological, and other conditions.

RISK AND UNCERTAINTY

We may gain a fuller understanding of the nature of uncertainty by examining a closely related concept—*risk*. For example, if experience has shown that there is on the average 1 fire per 100 docks in a harbor per year, then we say that the probability or risk of a fire to any one dock is $\frac{1}{100}$, or 1 per cent. Insurance rates are based on these types of risk.

In many situations involving risk, no nice and neat experience rates are available: Will a new product catch on? Is the planned venture likely to be successful? How close is a research project to payoff? What will future economic conditions be like? Answers to such questions involve evaluation primarily in terms of managerial judgment, even though objective data—trend projections, correlation analysis, other research—may be available to aid in this process. The plain, simple rates of the insurable type of risk are absent from these types of problems. The nature of the risk involved is not an insurable one, and we call it *uncertainty*.

As a further distinction, we may consider insurable risks as *objective*, in the sense that they are based on rates taken from adequate past experience, with the expectation that future conditions will yield essentially the same rates. On the other hand, if a market director says, "I feel that there is an 80 per cent chance that the coming sales season will be one of heavy demand," he is talking primarily of *subjective* probability, based primarily on his judgment of future uncertainty even though his judgment will be supported by experience in similar situations in the past and various economic and other forecasts. The joint judgment, obtained by consensus or by averaging percentage estimates of individuals comprising a group—such as all district sales managers—is also a subjective probability.

Is it valid to treat an opinion, such as a research director's estimate that there is a 75 per cent likelihood that a certain study will lead to a new, successfully marketable product, as a probability? Probability, in the classic sense, depends on verifiable past outcomes—the throws of unbiased dice or the life-expectancy rates of insurance companies. An opinion, on the other hand, is based on experience in situations similar to the situation at hand. The judgments and weights exist primarily in the mind of the opinion maker and are scarcely verifiable in an objective way. Whether the opinion maker's judgment can be considered a kind of probability or not is a question that may engage philosophers, but it is of small concern in practice. If we do not have objective risk data, we have no recourse but to use subjective probability.

OBJECTIVE PROBABILITY

Examine the toss of two unbiased coins. The various possible outcomes may be visualized in the form of a "probability tree" (see Figure 11–1). Attaching probabilities of 50 per cent (or 0.5) to each individual toss (meaning that a head is just as likely as a tail), we obtain:

Probability of Outcome	Outcome
50% or 0.5	Head and Tail or Tail and Head
25% or 0.25	Both Heads
25% or 0.25	Both Tails

The total of these probabilities must add up to 100 per cent (or 1.0). The individual probabilities shown above may be considered the *expected* outcomes for the next toss of two coins or the next series of

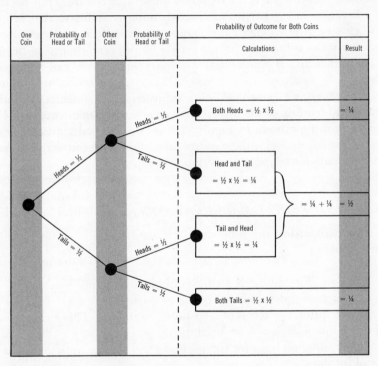

FIGURE 11-1. *Coin-tossing illustration of probability tree.* The possible outcomes from the throw of 2 coins, shown in diagram form, resemble a tree—hence the term *tree diagram* or *probability tree.* For 2 coins the probabilities are: Both heads or both tails—$\frac{1}{2} \times \frac{1}{2} = \frac{1}{4}$. Head-tail combinations—$\frac{1}{2} \times \frac{1}{2} + \frac{1}{2} \times \frac{1}{2} = \frac{1}{4} + \frac{1}{4} = \frac{1}{2}$. Extensions to 3 or more coins are apparent. (From Enrick, *Management Planning.* Copyright © 1967 by McGraw-Hill, Inc. Used by permission of McGraw-Hill Book Company.)

tosses, even though the *actual* distribution of outcomes may differ. Our interest, however, centers around expectations—particularly when a bet is being made.

SUBJECTIVE PROBABILITY

Let us now look at a business venture. We feel that a new synthetic material has a good market potential, and it is estimated that with our research resources we have an 80 per cent chance of success. Only one other firm has the resources for similar research. But because of differences in the particular research skills available to that firm, it is likely to utilize a somewhat different approach from ours, which our research staff estimates as having only a 70 per cent chance of success. Pilot studies and literature searches have further confirmed our estimates.

Although we now deal with subjective probabilities, it seems sound and feasible to use the subjective values in a manner parallel to the coin-tossing procedure. Figure 11–2 shows the results, giving the expected outcomes. Next, these outcomes may be invested with cost and profit calculations as an aid to decision making.

COST AND PROFIT CALCULATIONS

We will utilize the following simplified cost and profit data for our evaluations:

1. Cost of the research, to us, is estimated at $4 million.
2. Successful development of the new synthetic material should be worth $10 million in terms of sales profit attainable. This estimate and all other financial data have been discounted to present value so as to provide a common basis for comparison regardless of anticipated futurity of incomes.
3. Because of legal requirements, we know we will not have a monopoly if we succeed and our competitor fails. We will have to license the process to him at an expected gain to us of $2 million. Conversely, if we fail but he succeeds, we may obtain a license from him at that figure.

From these data, we can determine the financial effects of the possible outcomes as follows:

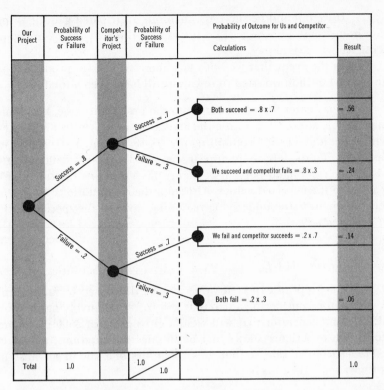

Our Project	Probability of Success or Failure	Compet- itor's Project	Probability of Success or Failure	Probability of Outcome for Us and Competitor	
				Calculations	Result
			Success = .7	Both succeed = .8 x .7	= .56
	Success = .8		Failure = .3	We succeed and competitor fails = .8 x .3	= .24
	Failure = .2		Success = .7	We fail and competitor succeeds = .2 x .7	= .14
			Failure = .3	Both fail = .2 x .3	= .06
Total	1.0	1.0 1.0			1.0

FIGURE 11–2. *Probability tree for business venture.* We and our principal competitor are working on a research project for a new synthetic material, each utilizing a different approach. Probabilities of research success or failure are given, based on the most competent opinions available. As in the coin-tossing example (Figure 11–1), the expected outcomes are obtained by successive multiplications along the probability tree. For example, there is a $.8 \times .3 = .24$ (or 24 per cent) chance that we will succeed (probability of 8 per cent) *and* that our competitor will fail (probability of 3 per cent). (From Enrick, *Management Planning.* Copyright © 1967 by McGraw-Hill, Inc. Used by permission of McGraw-Hill Book Company.)

1. If we both succeed, neither will license the process from the other. Thus, sales profit of $10 million less research of $4 million gives a net gain of $6 million.

2. If we succeed and he fails, we get an additional $2 million for the process license, or a total gain of $8 million.

3. If we fail and he succeeds, then our anticipated gain of $6 million in outcome 1 above will be cut to $4 million by the $2-million license fee we have to pay.

4. In the event that we both fail, there will be no product to sell and the $4 million invested in research will have been a total loss.

We may enter these cost data into the probability tree, but a more manageable approach is to use the arrangement shown in Figure 11–3, with the middle section containing the $6, $8, $4, and $–4 million just discussed. To the left, there appear the probability-tree data of Figure 11–2. The right-hand portion of Figure 11–3 contains the calculations leading to the expected values. Although the computations as such are self-explanatory, the underlying reasoning involves the special concept of *expected value*.

EXPECTED VALUE

The concept of expected value may be illustrated by an example. A salesman is considering a trip that will cost $100, involving the possible sale of a generator that will yield a gross profit of $500 in commissions. Past experience shows that of 10 sales presentations, only 1 has led to a successful sale, so that the probability of a sale in this instance is 10 per cent. We thus have:

$$\text{Expected Gross Profit} = \$500 \times 0.1 = \$50$$

Further:

$$\text{Expected Value of Trip} = \text{Expected Gross Profit} - \text{Cost of Trip}$$
$$= \$50 - \$100$$
$$= -\$50$$

In other words, we expect a loss of $50, and the salesman should not make the trip.

Utilization of this principle is what leads to an expected value of $5.6 million for the synthetic-material research (Figure 11–3). If we are very lucky (the case where we are successful and the competitor fails), we will make much more than expectation (namely, $8 million), but there is also the chance of a loss of $4 million. The expected value means that in the long run, if we continue to use the type of approach for assessing uncertainty such as we have done, we will tend to "average out" to the expectations.

Admittedly, the concept has its drawbacks, because in the end we

		a	b	c	d	e	f	
		Success	Failure	Success	Failure	Success	Failure	Expected Value, in Millions of Dollars
		Probability (from tree diagram of Figure 11-2)		Competitor — Anticipated Profit to Us, in Millions of Dollars		Expected Profit to Us, in Millions of Dollars		
				*	*	a x c	b x d	e + f
Us	Success	.8 x .7 = .56	.8 x .3 = .24	6	8	.56 x 6 = 3.36	.24 x 8 = 1.92	5.28
	Failure	.2 x .7 = .14	.2 x .3 = .06	4	-4	.14 x 4 = .56	.06 x (-4) = -.24	.32
Total expected value to us								5.60

*Based on these data, in millions of dollars, discounted to present value terms: estimated research cost, 4; estimated sales profit, 10; license fee, 2. The latter is paid to us if we succeed and our competitor fails, or is paid by us if he succeeds and we fail. If both succeed or both fail, no license fee is involved—hence the net loss, −4.

FIGURE 11–3. Expected value of business venture. We and our principal competitor are working on a research project, each utilizing a different approach. By agreement, if one succeeds and the other fails, the one failing may purchase a license from the other for $2 million. Other anticipated costs and profits are as shown in the footnote to the figure. Adjustment of these values to allow for probabilities of success or failure results in the expected values shown. The total expected value of the venture to us is $5.6 million, but a maximum profit of $8 million or a loss of $4 million is possible. The expected value is the most likely profit. (From Enrick, Management Planning. Copyright © 1967 by McGraw-Hill, Inc. Used by permission of McGraw-Hill Book Company.)

	a	b	c	
Markup Strategies, Per Cent	State of Nature (Kind of Season)			
	Good	Fair	Poor	
	Anticipated Sales, $1,000 per Week			
10	100	50	20	
20	35	25	15	
30	30	20	10	

	Anticipated Profit, $1,000 per Week			
	= Markup x Anticipated Sales			
10	.10 x 100 = 10	.10 x 50 = 5	.10 x 20 = 2	
20	.20 x 35 = 7	.20 x 25 = 5	.20 x 15 = 3	
30	.30 x 30 = 9	.30 x 20 = 6	.30 x 10 = 3	

	Probability of Good, Fair, or Poor Season, Per Cent			Expected Value of Strategy, $1,000 per Week = a + b + c
	20	60	20	
	Expected Profit, $1,000 per Week = Probability x Anticipated Profit			
10	.2 x 10 = 2.0	.6 x 5 = 3.0	.2 x 2 = 0.4	2 + 3 + .4 = 5.4
20	.2 x 7 = 1.4	.6 x 5 = 3.0	.2 x 3 = 0.6	1.4 + 3 + .6 = 5.0
30	.2 x 9 = 1.8	.6 x 6 = 3.6	.2 x 3 = 0.6	1.8 + 3.6 + .6 = 6.0

FIGURE 11–4. *Expected value of three markup strategies.* Based on the data given, the markup of 30 per cent yields the highest expected value in terms of profit per week, namely, $6,000. (From Enrick, *Management Planning.* Copyright © 1967 by McGraw-Hill, Inc. Used by permission of McGraw-Hill Book Company.)

obtain individual outcomes, not average expectations. Nevertheless, the concept has practical value and is finding increasing uses. The value of the approach is that a logical system is available. Decisions based on this systematic framework are likely to be better decisions in the long run. Evidence is accumulating, indeed, that the gains attainable are real. See, for example, Figure 11–4, in which the concept is employed to determine the best of the three markup strategies. Figure 11–5 extends the tree diagram to three sets of probabilities.

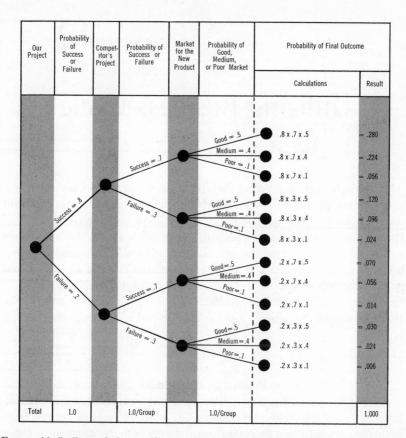

Our Project	Probability of Success or Failure	Competitor's Project	Probability of Success or Failure	Market for the New Product	Probability of Good, Medium, or Poor Market	Probability of Final Outcome	
						Calculations	Result
					Good = .5	.8 x .7 x .5	= .280
					Medium = .4	.8 x .7 x .4	= .224
			Success = .7		Poor = .1	.8 x .7 x .1	= .056
	Success = .8		Failure = .3		Good = .5	.8 x .3 x .5	= .120
					Medium = .4	.8 x .3 x .4	= .096
					Poor = .1	.8 x .3 x .1	= .024
					Good = .5	.2 x .7 x .5	= .070
			Success = .7		Medium = .4	.2 x .7 x .4	= .056
	Failure = .2				Poor = .1	.2 x .7 x .1	= .014
			Failure = .3		Good = .5	.2 x .3 x .5	= .030
					Medium = .4	.2 x .3 x .4	= .024
					Poor = .1	.2 x .3 x .1	= .006
Total	1.0		1.0/Group		1.0/Group		1.000

FIGURE 11–5. *Extended tree diagram for business venture.* Three sets of probabilities are involved: (1) our own efforts and their probable success or failure; (2) our competitor's efforts and their probable success or failure; and (3) the market for the new product and the probable market conditions, assuming that our efforts or our competitor's efforts are successful. (From Enrick, *Management Planning.* Copyright © 1967 by McGraw-Hill, Inc. Used by permission of McGraw-Hill Book Company.)

SUMMARY

Uncertainty surrounding planning calls for judicious application of subjective probabilities, within a logical framework that reviews the potential of various possible strategies in the light of probable business and other conditions. Ultimately, the greater insights thus afforded will result in a higher long-term quality of decisions.

CHAPTER 12

Utilizing Business-Cycle Indicators

The analysis and forecasting techniques presented thus far have emphasized the problems of the individual firm in anticipating sales and markets, by taking cognizance of competitive developments and by considering general tendencies and cycles within the firm's industry and market area. Over-all business and economic climate, as represented by the *business cycle,* has a considerable bearing on individual market and sales expectations. For the analysis and forecasting of business-cycle developments, the *indicator approach* pioneered by the National Bureau of Economic Research has found widespread acceptance.

DEFINING BUSINESS CYCLE

A *business cycle,* as defined by the Bureau, consists of "expansions occurring at about the same time in many economic activities, followed by similarly general recessions." It is noted that the contractions occurring are followed by revivals that merge into the expansion phase of the next cycle. The alternating and recurring movements of these cycles reflect over-all, or "aggregate," economic activity and not individual statistical series or mere seasonal fluctuations. Two essential ingredients go into the making of the business cycle:

1. Multitudinous economic activities cumulate into the over-all composite of the economy.
2. Eventually, forces working contrary to the general course of the economy gain sufficient strength to bring about a directional reversal of the cycle.

The turning points (or peaks and troughs) of the business cycle comprise the reference dates with regard to which we measure the length of expansion or contraction. Expansion represents the rise in business activity from trough to peak, and it usually covers from 2 to 3 years. Contraction, on the other hand, has generally occurred within less than 2 years, and often less than 1 year. These are general, "average" observations, which ignore some notable exceptions. In times of a strong growth trend in an economy, it is only natural that the expansionary phase would predominate.

COINCIDENT SERIES

The reference dates of the cycle permit us to identify individual series that are *coincident* in regard to peak and trough occurrences. For example, our firm's industry or market may have cyclical fluctuations that correspond with the turning points of the general business cycle. Such parallel series are not expected to be precisely coincident, but roughly so. Within an economy at large, the following individual series are approximately coincident: gross national product, personal income, industrial production, nonagricultural employment, unemployment rate, commodity wholesale-price index (excluding farm products and foods). Again, there are instances of noncoincidence.

LEADING SERIES

Because of their predictive value, leading series are of great interest. For these series, the turning points typically precede the reference dates that mark the peaks and troughs of the general business cycle. Known as *leading indicators,* these series relate primarily to future production and employment. Included in this group are such measures as manufacturers' new orders for durable goods, the average workweek in manufacturing, the start of housing construction, corporate profits after taxes, common-stock prices, and spot prices for industrial materials.

Unfortunately, these indicators do not always lead an upswing or a downturn. Moreover, it is often difficult to interpret their meaning, particularly when various series do not show highly marked patterns or, as often happens, when there is some inconsistency or contradiction among the leading indicators. With experience and judgment and by using various other business and economic data for support, analysts of business cycles feel that they can come up with good predictions. Unfortunately, consensus among analysts may be lacking, and just because one analyst has been right in his predictions for a long period of time does not mean that he will be right in the future.

30 Leading Indicators

1. Average workweek of production workers, manufacturing
2. Accession rate, manufacturing
3. Layoff rate, manufacturing
4. Number of persons on temporary layoff, all industries
5. Average weekly initial claims for unemployment insurance, state programs
6. Value of manufacturers' new orders, durable-goods industries
7. New private nonfarm dwelling units started
8. Construction contracts awarded for commercial and industrial buildings, floor space
9. Contracts and orders for plant and equipment
10. Newly approved capital appropriations, 1,000 manufacturing corporations
11. Net change in the business population, operating businesses
12. Number of new business incorporations
13. Current liabilities of business failures
14. Number of business failures with liabilities of $100,000 and over
15. Corporate profits after taxes
16. Price per unit of labor cost index
17. Profits (before taxes) per dollar of sales, all manufacturing corporations
18. Index of stock prices, 500 common stocks
19. Change in book value of manufacturers' inventories of materials and supplies
20. Change in business inventories, farm and nonfarm, after valuation adjustment
21. Ratio of profits to income originating, corporate, all industries
22. Index of industrial-materials prices
23. Value of manufacturers' new orders, machinery and equipment industries
24. Change in manufacturers' unfilled orders, durable-goods industries
25. Buying policy—production materials, percentage reporting commitments 60 days or longer
26. Index of new private housing units authorized by local building permits
27. Nonagricultural placements, all industries
28. Change in book value of manufacturing and trade inventories, total
29. Vendor performance, percentage reporting slower deliveries
30. Percentage reporting higher inventories of purchased materials

15 Roughly Coincident Indicators

1. Unemployment rate, married males, spouse present
2. Number of employees in nonagricultural establishments
3. Total nonagricultural employment, labor-force survey
4. Unemployment rate, total
5. Average weekly insured unemployment rate, state programs
6. Index of help-wanted advertising in newspapers
7. Index of industrial production
8. Gross national product in current dollars
9. Gross national product in 1954 dollars
10. Bank debits outside New York City, 343 centers
11. Personal income
12. Labor income in mining, manufacturing, and construction
13. Sales of retail stores
14. Index of wholesale prices, all commodities, other than farm products and foods
15. Final sales

7 Lagging Indicators

1. Business expenditures on new plant and equipment, total
2. Index of labor cost per unit of output, total manufacturing
3. Book value of manufacturers' inventories, all manufacturing industries
4. Book value of manufacturers' inventories of finished goods, all manufacturing industries
5. Consumer installment debt
6. Bank rates on short-term business loans, 19 cities
7. Index of labor cost per dollar of real corporate gross national product

Nevertheless, the use of leading indicators will *in the long run* aid the intelligent and sagacious businessman in better forecasting and thus superior planning than would otherwise be possible. It seems unlikely, moreover, that there will ever be a sure-fire method of calling the turns in the business cycle. The discriminating forecaster is therefore always a wary individual, who knows that no period of expansion or contraction ever repeats itself identically in duration, intensity or causation.

LAGGING SERIES

In a number of important economic series, it has been observed that peaks and troughs typically follow the turning points in general business. Included in this group are plant and equipment expenditures, manufacturers' inventories, and bank interest rates on business loans. Although they fall behind the general level of business activity. *lagging series* do have some predictive value. For example, a firm that is interested in expanding and needs to borrow funds should be aware that interest rates are likely to go up some time after a coincident-series peak has been reached. On the other hand, if a trough has occurred, interest rates are likely to reach their low point some weeks later. Borrowing policy of the firm can then be planned accordingly.

There are also many businesses which experience fluctuations in demands parallel to lagging series, and this information is useful in making short-term predictions.

SOURCES OF DATA

Information regarding current economic indicators can be obtained monthly from the publication *Business Cycle Developments,* prepared by the Bureau of the Census of the United States Department of Commerce. A variety of types of data series appear in this periodical (details of which are given in Chapter 13). The indicators provided in this government periodical are listed in Table 12–1.

THE VALUE OF THE INDICATORS

Economic indicators tend to lead or lag by weeks and rarely by more than a few months. Therefore, their principal value lies in short-range prediction. Decisions on buildup of inventories in anticipation of rising market demand or on cutbacks in production when depressed sales outlook threatens, as well as a great deal of other short-term planning, must be based on reliable short-range forecasts. In this predictive endeavor, the leading indicators will be of considerable value. Their information content, used wisely by the planner, will enhance the quality of his decisions.

Firms involved in large-scale production and sales operations are particularly vulnerable to fluctuations in demand; typical examples are the automobile, appliance, and petroleum-products firms, as well as certain textile firms, where extensive use is made of leading indicators. Multiple correlation analysis, a technique presented in Chapter 7, is also useful in determining how the information contained in economic indicators should be employed in forecasting an individual firm's sales. The method utilizes past data as follows:

1. Observe the firm's sales experience of the past 2–3 years. If the firm markets a variety of distinct products, it may be desirable to break down all data by product categories for each major market.

2. Next, using past data of leading indicators, correlate the values of the indicators with subsequent actual sales 3, 4, 5, and more weeks ahead, as may be appropriate. The selection of the particular time advance will depend on the planning and forecasting needs of the firm; but it must be realized that, generally, the shorter the gap between time periods the better the correlation is likely to be.

3. From the correlation analysis, the relative importance of each of the 30 indicators in relation to the firm's future sales anticipation will have been observed. Some indicators will be of primary importance and others of secondary significance. Some 10–20 indicators may be primary, some 5–15 may be secondary, and the remainder will be of tertiary or no relevance.

4. For the primary and secondary indicators, the data from the correlation analysis will also yield a prediction equation.

5. Use the prediction equation for future forecasting.

As with all forecasting techniques, the *prediction equation* will be in need of periodic review and may require revision with changing market and other ancillary conditions. Again, the prediction obtained is not to be taken as more than an aid, with executive judgment in the light of all known factors providing the final arbiter of the decisions to be made.

In a sense, all of the economic, social, and political developments of a society are indicators, or trends and portents of sales climate and market potentials to be anticipated by the individual business firm. Among the multitudes of figures, data, analyses, and reports that are becoming available daily, weekly, monthly, and at various other time intervals, some of the more important ones for most business forecasting needs will be presented in Chapter 13.

SUMMARY

Business cycles affect the anticipations of practically every business firm and operation in a country. In past decades, little was known about the nature of these cycles and still less about their portents. In recent years, however, great strides have been made in analyzing cycles, in developing theories about their nature, and in coming up with useful and timely practical data that are of great value in short-range forecasting. The business cycle need not be accepted passively. Rather, business operations and related economic actions can be planned, based on the information provided by indicators and other data and on the judgment of the executives, managers, and other people involved in the decision-making process.

CHAPTER 13

Obtaining Published Forecasting Data

A wide variety of published information is available to the forecaster, concerning not only the economy and business conditions in general, but also specific market areas. The most numerous, useful, and up-to-date series are published by the government. A number of private foundations, university bureaus of business research, and trade associations also collect and publish information of value for evaluating sales expectations and market potentials.

NONGOVERNMENTAL SOURCES

Sources other than governmental include numerous trade groups and a number of private organizations that supply specialized information within certain market and industry areas. Often, the infrequency and thus the problem of up-to-dateness of the material detract from the usefulness of such publications.

Survey Research Center

A widely used source of information is the annually published survey on consumer finances prepared by the Survey Research Center, Institute for Social Research of the University of Michigan at Ann Arbor. Business firms and banks, which support the research by their subscriptions, obtain quarterly reports from the Center.

F. W. Dodge Corporation

Some current data series collected privately, such as compilations on new-construction starts prepared by the F. W. Dodge Corporation, in New York, are used in governmental series. In fact, since new construction is usually quite important as an indicator of prosperous business conditions, this privately prepared but widely published series receives considerable attention by forecasters.

The Brookings Institution

The Brookings Institution in Washington, D.C., is a "nonprofit, nonpartisan" organization engaged in research, education, and publication in economics, government, foreign policy, and social sciences. Many of the Institution's publications have significant bearing on general market conditions.

Committee for Economic Development

The Committee for Economic Development, in New York, consisting of 200 trustees drawn from the ranks of industry board chairmen, financial institutions, and university presidents, and aided by an advisory board of scholars, conducts research and prepares policy recommendations on major economic issues. Employment rates, living standards, economic growth, and economic stability are general areas of the Committee's scope which will be of general background interest to forecasters. Economic Base Reports, prepared by the Committee's Associate Centers for specific areas, contain data on land use, specific industry status, work force, and "profiles" of executive groups.

GOVERNMENTAL SOURCES

The principal governmental publications likely to be of interest are summarized in this section. A great many more sources could have been given, but the purpose here is not to overwhelm but merely to identify those most pertinent to market and sales forecasting. The publications included contain a fair amount of overlap in types of data, so that a decision on subscribing to any of them should take this factor into account.

Marketing Information Guide

SOURCE: U.S. Department of Commerce, Business and Defense Services Administration (BDSA). Obtainable by subscription from Superintendent of Documents, U.S. Government Printing Office, Washington, D.C., or from field offices of the U.S. Department of Commerce.

FREQUENCY OF PUBLICATION: Monthly.

NATURE OF MATERIAL: An annotated bibliography of current periodical articles, books, and booklets providing both general and specific marketing information. A typical issue may contain from 200 to 400 separate entries. There is also an annual subject index. The purpose is to "serve the domestic and foreign marketing informational needs of those engaged in or concerned with the sale or purchase of industrial or consumer products and business or personal services." The following topics are covered: marketing functions, policy, methodology, and operations; market area data, United States and international; market data regarding consumers, government, industrial, and institutional users; information on industries and commodities (including agriculture, forestry, and fishing) , mining, construction, manufacture, transportation, communication and utilities, wholesale and retail trades, finance, insurance, and real estate.

Survey of Current Business

SOURCE: U.S. Department of Commerce, Office of Business Economics, Washington, D.C. Obtainable by subscription from Superintendent of Documents, U.S. Government Printing Office, Washington, D.C.

FREQUENCY OF PUBLICATION: Quarterly.

NATURE OF MATERIAL: Two of the most widely used measures of total economic activity are published: gross national product (GNP) , and national income (NI) . GNP reflects total expenditures or market value of total output, while NI represents the factor costs—the earnings of labor and property—in producing this output.

A forecast of total GNP is derived by estimating expenditures on final output made by each of these four broad purchasing groups:

1. Consumers, or "Personal Consumption Expenditures," including individuals and nonprofit institutions: purchases of durable goods, such as household equipment and automobiles; expenditures on nondurable goods, chiefly clothing and food; outlays for services, such as rent, domestic help, transportation, and medical care, as well as the rental value of owner-occupied homes.

2. Business, or "Gross Private Domestic Investment," including private firms and nonprofit organizations; investment in residential and nonresidential structures; investment in producers' durable equipment, such as machinery and equipment.

3. Foreign, or "Net Exports of Goods and Services," reflecting the excess of sales abroad over imports.

4. Government, or "Government Purchases of Goods and Services," at the federal, state, and local levels.

Changes in the structure of the economy are revealed from a study of the various components of the NI accounts, as follows:

1. Corporate profits: This is the most volatile series, hence highly significant for forecasting purposes. Both before- and after-tax data are given, as well as dividends and retained earnings.

2. Proprietors' income: Individually owned firms, partnerships, and noncorporate enterprises comprise this sector of the economy. Incomes are broken down by business and professional and farming sources.

3. Compensation of employees: Wages and salaries plus "supplements" primarily in the form of social insurance and private pension funds make up by far the greatest part of national income.

4. Rental income of persons: Rental on real property, net rental value of owner-occupied houses, royalties received from patents and other rights, and certain "net interest" from private business make up this series.

A distinction must be made between national income (NI) and personal income: the latter excludes contributions for social insurance and corporate profits; but it does include dividend payments, net interest paid by government, interest paid by consumers, and certain "transfer payments" such as social-security benefits, veterans' bonuses, and corporate gifts to nonprofit institutions. Thus "personal income" measures income received by individuals, unincorporated firms, and nonprofit organizations. Forecasters are particularly interested in data on "disposable personal income," found by deducting personal taxes (such as income and estate) from total personal income. When "personal outlays" are subtracted from the latter income, an estimate of current personal savings is obtained. Disposable personal income and propensity to save are significant indicators of consumer sales to be anticipated.

Manufacturers' Shipments, Inventories and Orders

SOURCE: U.S. Department of Commerce, Bureau of the Census, Washington, D.C. Obtainable by subscription from Superintendent of Documents, U.S. Government Printing Office, Washington, D.C.

FREQUENCY OF PUBLICATION: Monthly.

NATURE OF MATERIAL: Detailed data series, both with and without seasonal adjustment, are brought for the following:

1. Value of manufacturers' shipments, inventories, and orders: This information is broken down by 50 industry groups and subgroups. Both new and unfilled orders are given.

2. Regrouping of data on value of manufacturers' shipments, inventories, and orders by market series: Breakdowns include home goods and apparel; consumer staples; equipment and defense products, except automotive; automotive equipment; construction materials, supplies, and intermediate products; other materials and supplies; and supplementary series on consumer durables, defense products, machinery and equipment industries.

3. Analysis of data above in terms of month-to-month and long-term changes: The evaluation includes average rise and decline, as percentages, for the following periods: monthly, 3-months, 6-months, annual, and 5-year.

4. Supplementary and often highly useful analyses are derived from the basic data series, such as ratio of inventories to shipments and unfilled orders and value of inventories by stage of fabrication. An example appears in Table 13–1.

Business Cycle Developments

SOURCE: U.S. Department of Commerce, Bureau of the Census, Washington, D.C. Obtainable by subscription from Superintendent of Documents, U.S. Government Printing Office, Washington, D.C., or from field offices of the U.S. Department of Commerce.

FREQUENCY OF PUBLICATION: Monthly.

NATURE OF MATERIAL: A current analysis of business conditions, summarizing many of the available economic time series in convenient form for short-term evaluation and interpretation, thereby supplementing other reports by the Department of Commerce. Special features include the following:

1. The various data series are arranged according to their usual timing relations during the course of the business cycle.

2. Special analytical measures and historical cyclical comparisons are provided, designed to help in evaluating the current stage of the business cycle.

3. There is a high degree of timeliness, accomplished by means of accelerated data collection and assembly, electronic processing and evaluation, and early publication. As a result, *Business Cycle Developments* is published on the 22nd of each month, bringing data for the preceding month.

About 90 principal indicators with more than 300 components are used. The chief series are listed in Table 12–1 of the preceding chap-

TABLE 13–1. RATIO OF MANUFACTURERS' INVENTORIES TO SHIPMENTS
AND UNFILLED ORDERS TO SHIPMENTS, BY INDUSTRY GROUP
(BASED ON SEASONALLY ADJUSTED DATA)

	Inventories–Shipments Ratio				Unfilled Orders–Shipments Ratio[1] (Months' Backlog)			
Industry Group	September 1966[p]	August 1966[r]	July 1966	September 1965	September 1966[p]	August 1966[r]	July 1966	September 1965
All manufacturing industries, total	1.70	1.68	1.65	1.65	2.98	2.89	2.83	2.66
Durable-goods industries, total	2.07	2.05	1.99	1.97	3.65	3.54	3.49	3.23
Stone, clay, and glass products	1.70	1.79	1.80	1.69	(NA)	(NA)	(NA)	(NA)
Primary metals	1.76	1.76	1.68	1.92	1.88	1.85	1.82	1.68
Fabricated metals	2.31	2.31	2.26	2.39	3.00	3.14	3.12	2.88
Machinery, except electrical	2.80	2.77	2.71	2.69	3.68	3.64	3.51	3.10
Electrical machinery	2.12	2.07	1.96	2.11	3.55	3.49	3.31	3.35
Transportation equipment	1.79	1.76	1.74	1.49	7.96	7.40	7.71	6.71
Instruments and related products	2.54	2.42	2.40	2.47	(NA)	(NA)	(NA)	(NA)
Nondurable-goods industries, total	1.29	1.28	1.28	1.30	0.61	0.62	0.61	0.64
Food and kindred products	0.86	0.85	0.90	0.86	(X)	(X)	(X)	(X)
Tobacco products	5.46	5.53	5.67	5.51	(X)	(X)	(X)	(X)
Textile-mill products	1.95	1.94	1.92	1.92	(NA)	(NA)	(NA)	(NA)
Paper and allied products	1.17	1.16	1.14	1.18	(NA)	(NA)	(NA)	(NA)
Chemicals and allied products	1.55	1.50	1.46	1.45	(X)	(X)	(X)	(X)
Petroleum and coal products	1.05	1.06	1.04	1.05	(X)	(X)	(X)	(X)
Rubber and plastics products, n.e.c.	1.32	1.28	1.25	1.33	(X)	(X)	(X)	(X)

[p] Preliminary.
[r] Revised.
(NA) Not available.
(X) Not applicable.
[1] Excludes the following industries with no unfilled-order backlogs: wooden containers; glass containers; metal cans, barrels and drums; motor-vehicle assembly operations; foods and related products; tobacco; apparel and related products; chemicals; petroleum and coal products; and rubber and plastics products, n.e.c.

Editor's note: The significance of these ratios for the anticipation of business conditions is well recognized. For example, when the inventories–shipments ratio is high, we may anticipate slowdowns in production until the ratio becomes more balanced; on the other hand, large backlogs of unfilled orders presage a period of increased activity, until supply catches up with the demand indicated.

SOURCE: *Manufacturers' Shipments, Inventories and Orders,* published monthly by the U.S. Department of Commerce, Bureau of the Census, Washington, D.C.

ter. Movements of each time series are shown against the background of expansion or contraction of the general business cycle, so that "leads" and "lags" can be readily detected and unusual cyclical developments spotted. The classification of the series and the business-cycle turning dates are those designed by the National Bureau of Economic Research, which pioneered this approach.

Federal Reserve Bulletin

SOURCE: Board of Governors of the Federal Reserve System, Washington, D.C.

FREQUENCY OF PUBLICATION: Monthly.

NATURE OF MATERIAL: Numerous statistical series, but the data of prime interest to forecasters of general business activity and specific industry developments is the Index of Industrial Production. Although the index includes only manufacturing, mining, gas and electric utilities (or only a little more than one-third of the total value of GNP), it nevertheless is timely (data are published monthly with a time lag of only about 15 days) and covers those parts of the economy that are often considered most sensitive to changes in over-all demand. Minerals, finished and semi-finished goods, and utility output are used by all other sectors of the economy, thereby making the index a useful barometer of changes in business activity.

Comprised of some 200 individual series, the index is classified in two separate ways:

1. Industrial groupings (using designations defined in the U.S. Budget Bureau's "Standard Industrial Classification Manual").
2. Market groupings: The individual series are combined into industry or market subgroups which, in turn, are grouped into major subdivisions.

The buildup from small sectors to major groups is shown for the two classifications in Figures 13–1 and 13–2 (p. 102).

The monthly detail is of considerable service in analyzing demand and supply developments at various stages in the production process, and thus in making forecasts.

Long Term Economic Growth

SOURCE: U.S. Department of Commerce, Bureau of the Census, Washington, D.C.

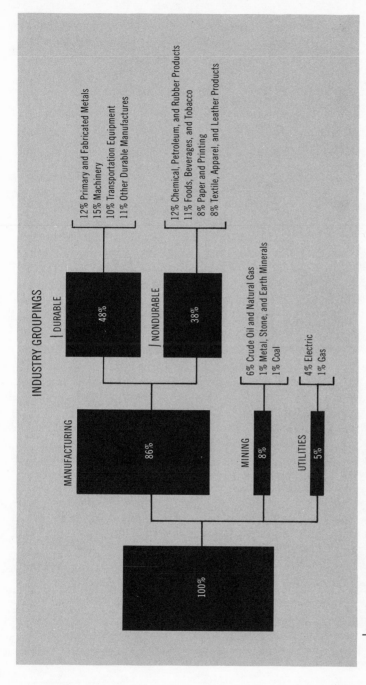

FIGURE 13–1. *Federal Reserve Index of Industrial Production by industry groupings.* (From *Keys to Business Forecasting*, Federal Reserve Bank, Richmond, Virginia.)

101

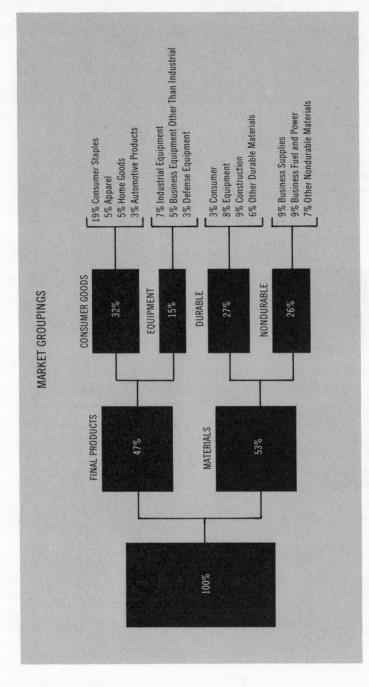

MARKET GROUPINGS

FINAL PRODUCTS 47%

CONSUMER GOODS 32%
19% Consumer Staples
5% Apparel
5% Home Goods
3% Automotive Products

EQUIPMENT 15%
7% Industrial Equipment
5% Business Equipment Other Than Industrial
3% Defense Equipment

100%

MATERIALS 53%

DURABLE 27%
3% Consumer
8% Equipment
9% Construction
6% Other Durable Materials

NONDURABLE 26%
9% Business Supplies
9% Business Fuel and Power
7% Other Nondurable Materials

Note: Details may not add to totals because of rounding.

FIGURE 13–2. *Federal Reserve Index of Industrial Production by market groupings.* (From *Keys to Business Forecasting,* Federal Reserve Bank, Richmond, Virginia.)

FREQUENCY OF PUBLICATION: Probably every several years. Only one issue has appeared so far, covering the period from 1860 to 1965.

NATURE OF MATERIAL: Brings together about 400 aggregate annual economic time series and nearly 800 component series useful for studying economic-development patterns and projecting future trends. Organized in five major parts, this compendium brings:

1. Measures of economic growth, such as output of goods and services, potential output, input of different human and material factors, and productivity.

2. Factors vitally related to growth, such as education, research and development, and health; together with background economic processes such as prices, interest rates, savings, wages, profits, debts, assets of financial institutions, balance of international payments, monetary gold stock, use of labor and capital, and seasonal and cyclical forces.

3. Very long-range regional and industry growth trends. Regions and industries that are undergoing the most rapid rates of change are spotlighted.

4. A comparison of U.S. growth with that of six major foreign countries.

5. Growth-rate comparisons over a variety of time spans.

In the appendix, a description of the various series is provided. Basic source data are given. Aside from government agencies, such distinguished private research groups as the National Bureau of Economic Research, the Committee for Economic Development, and the Brookings Institution provide source data. Governmental sources include the Office of Business Economics of the Department of Commerce, the Bureau of Labor Statistics of the Department of Labor, and the Board of Governors of the Federal Reserve System.

For typical examples of the kind of data provided, see Figures 13-3 (p. 104), 13-4 (p. 105), and 13-5 (p. 106).

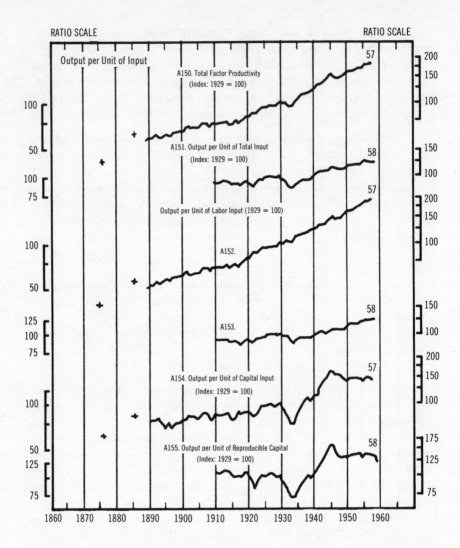

Figure 13–3. *Long-term growth in productivity*. Changes in aggregate national output are shown in terms of output per unit of labor and capital combined and in terms of output per man-hour, per employee, and per unit of capital separately. (From *Long Term Economic Growth*, U.S. Department of Commerce, Bureau of the Census, Washington, D.C.)

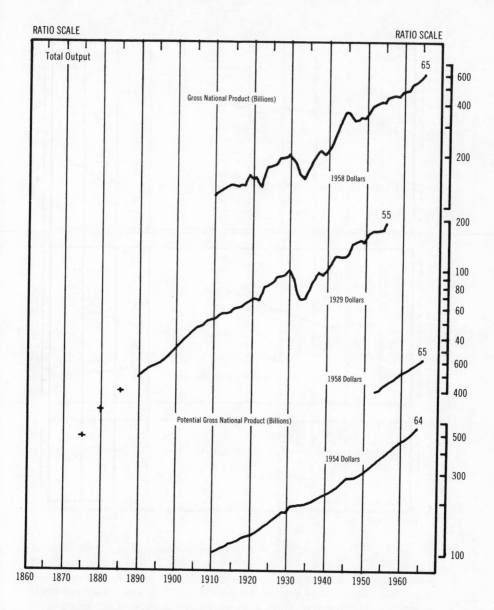

FIGURE 13–4. *Long-term growth in gross national product.* The GNP is the primary measure of national economic growth. (From *Long Term Economic Growth,* U.S. Department of Commerce, Bureau of the Census, Washington, D.C.)

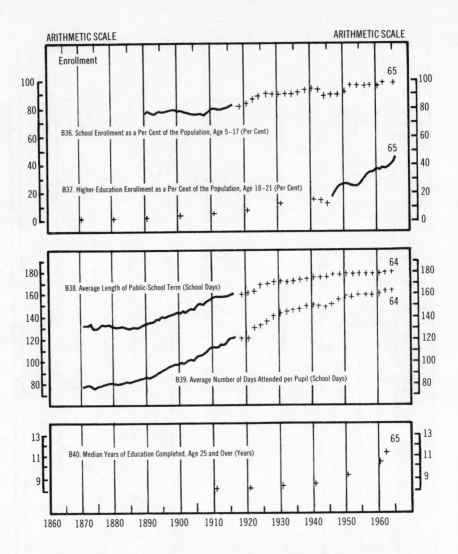

FIGURE 13-5. *Processes related to economic growth.* This figure indicates the educational preparation of the population in the United States, with its implications in terms of demand for additional education, ability to handle complex and demanding work, shifts in consumer interests for recreational and other leisure-time activities. Increased educational level will serve to increase the potential for productivity. (From *Long Term Economic Growth,* U.S. Department of Commerce, Bureau of the Census, Washington, D.C.)

TABLE 13–2. PRINCIPAL REPORTS OF THE BUREAU OF LABOR STATISTICS*

Report	Frequency of Publication
Area Wage Surveys	irregularly
Consumer Expenditures and Income	irregularly
Consumer Price Index	monthly
Current Wage Developments	semiannually
Daily Index of Spot Market Prices	daily
Industry Studies of Productivity, Technology and Related Economic Trends	irregularly
Monthly Labor Review	monthly
National Survey of Professional, Administrative, Technical and Clerical Pay	annually
Net Spendable Earnings	monthly
Productivity	irregularly
Retail Food Prices by Cities	monthly
Special Labor Force Reports	10 per year
Wages and Industrial Relations	every 5–8 weeks
Wholesale Price Index, Over-All	weekly
Wholesale Price Indexes, Detailed	monthly
Work Stoppages	monthly

* This listing represents merely a selection of what are believed to be the principal reports for the purpose of market and sales forecasting or related studies. A total of more than 50 titles, published by the Bureau at various regular and irregular intervals, serve a large variety of business and governmental needs. For a more detailed description, consult the source of Table 13–3.

Reports of the Bureau of Labor Statistics

SOURCE: U.S. Department of Labor, Bureau of Labor Statistics, Washington, D.C.

FREQUENCY OF PUBLICATION: Shown in Table 13–2 for the various bulletins, papers, reviews, and summaries represented.

NATURE OF MATERIAL: The following are the principal items that would be most likely to interest the forecaster:

1. Manpower and employment: Labor force, monthly and special reports, employees on nonagricultural payrolls, hours and earnings, labor turnover, scientific and technical personnel in industry and in state and local governments, and other series. Not only the availability of manpower for a firm, but also the likely market size for its output are generally dependent on developments reported under the "manpower and employment" categories.

TABLE 13–3. SUMMARY OF PRICE INDEXES PUBLISHED BY THE BUREAU OF LABOR STATISTICS

Program	Coverage	Source of Data	Detail of Data Available	Special Characteristics	Uses
Consumer Price Index	All goods and services purchased for living by urban wage earners and clerical workers, including single persons.	Sample of 1,775 food stores; 40,000 tenants; 16,000 other reporters. 56 cities in sample. Food and a few other items priced monthly in all cities; other items priced monthly in 5 largest cities, quarterly in other cities (on a rotating basis). Most pricing by personal interview; some by mail.	Indexes for all items and major groups and subgroups for U.S. and 23 large cities for urban wage earners and clerical workers, including single persons. Indexes for selected items, U.S. average. Retail prices and indexes of individual food items. Retail prices and indexes of fuels and electricity. Purchasing power of dollar, U.S. average.	Price index based on constant market basket. Based on expenditure patterns of about 5,000 wage-earner and clerical-worker consumer units in 1960–1961, beginning January 1964. Based on prices of about 400 items. Measures trend, not level of prices. Not a measure of intercity differences in living costs.	Economic measure of price movements. Wage escalation. Wage negotiations. Deflation of earnings to provide measures of real earnings. Measure of purchasing power of dollar at consumer level. Escalation of rental lease agreements and money payments from trust funds, wills, and so on.
Wholesale Price Index	All commodities in primary markets in U.S. including imports.	7,000 price quotations at first commercial transaction; mail survey. Also trade and government sources.	Prices and indexes for 2,600 products and product groupings. Indexes for 27 special groupings, 34 groupings by stage of processing, 8 groupings by durability of product. Indexes for all commodities combined and for selected subdivisions.	Commodity, not industry, classification. Variation in representation of commodities used in index. Measures price change, not level of prices. Effect of quality change not completely eliminated.	Economic measure of price movements. Measure of purchasing power of dollar at primary markets. Escalation in long-term contracts. LIFO accounting by some organizations.
Daily Index of Spot Market Prices	22 selected commodities.	Trade and government sources.	Prices for 33 individual specifications. Indexes for all commodities combined and for 6 special groupings.	Shows movement of prices of highly sensitive commodities.	Economic measure of price movements.
Industry-Sector Price Indexes	52 industries.	Price indexes included in Wholesale Price Index.	Indexes for 52 industries (8 mining and 44 manufacturing). Indexes for 141 5-digit product groups.	Industry, not commodity, classification. Secondary products included. Commodity indexes combined with industry weights.	Measures of industry price trends. Deflators for derivation of industry "real" output.

SOURCE: *Major BLS Programs—A Summary of Their Characteristics,* 1967; published annually by the Bureau of Labor Statistics, Washington, D.C.

2. Wages and industrial relations: Occupational wages by areas and industries with various breakdowns for professional, administrative, technical, and clerical categories. Wage scales and indexes. Industrial-relations data; health, insurance, and pension plans. Information under these headings supplements the manpower data.

3. Productivity, technology, and growth: Output per man-hour, studies of major technological innovations and their effect on broad sectors of the economy, long-range economic-growth projections, and interindustry employment tables.

4. Prices and living conditions: Consumer-expenditure surveys, consumer and wholesale price indexes, industry-sector price indexes, and other data of value in forecasting markets and price anticipations. See Table 13–3 for an example of the care and detail which go into the Bureau's programs.

Because of the many state and area breakdowns, the data are useful also for market-area analyses.

Economic Indicators

SOURCE: Council of Economic Advisers of the Joint Economic Committee of Congress, Washington, D.C.

FREQUENCY OF PUBLICATION: Monthly.

NATURE OF MATERIAL: A compilation, from numerous and diverse public and private data series, of important economic developments. Monthly data are given for the immediately preceding 13-month period. Otherwise, annual totals are provided. Several examples of data are given in Figures 13–6 (p. 111), 13–7 (p. 112), and 13–8 (p. 113). A survey of the table of contents will reveal the coverage:

Total Output, Income, and Spending
The Nation's Income, Expenditure, and Saving
Gross National Product or Expenditure
National Income
Sources of Personal Income
Disposition of Personal Income
Farm Income
Corporate Profits
Gross Private Domestic Investment
Expenditures for New Plant and Equipment

Employment, Unemployment, and Wages
Status of the Labor Force
Selected Measures of Unemployment and Part-Time Employment
Unemployment Insurance Programs
Nonagricultural Employment
Weekly Hours of Work—Selected Industries
Average Hourly and Weekly Earnings —Selected Industries
Production and Business Activity
Industrial Production

Production of Selected Manufactures

Weekly Indicators of Production

New Construction

New Housing Starts and Applications for Financing

Business Sales and Inventories—Total and Trade

Manufacturers' Shipments, Inventories, and New Orders

Merchandise Exports and Imports

U.S. Exports and Imports of Goods and Services

U.S. Balance of International Payments

Prices

Consumer Prices

Wholesale Prices

Prices Received and Paid by Farmers

Money, Credit, and Security Markets

Money Supply

Selected Liquid Assets Held by the Public

Bank Loans, Investments, Debits, and Reserves

Consumer and Real Estate Credit

Bond Yields and Interest Rates

Common Stock Prices, Yield, and Earnings

Federal Finance

Federal Administrative Budget Receipts and Expenditures

Federal Cash Receipts from and Payments to the Public

Federal Budget, National Income Accounts Basis

SUMMARY

A wealth of data series is published continually and with a relatively high degree of up-to-dateness. The forecaster should be familiar with the principal sources, as identified and described briefly in this chapter. For each market area and industry, however, additional information can be gathered from private groups, particularly from trade associations.

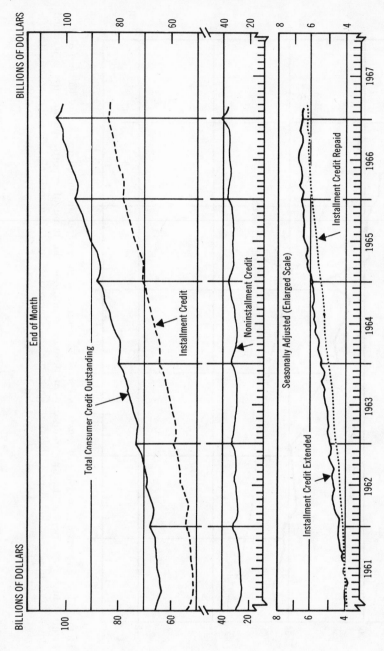

FIGURE 13-6. *Consumer credit outstanding.* Noninstallment credit represents primarily real estate. When installment credit increases unduly, a subsequent considerable slowdown, with its effects on business activity, may be anticipated. (From *Economic Indicators*, Council of Economic Advisers of the Joint Economic Committee of Congress, Washington, D.C.)

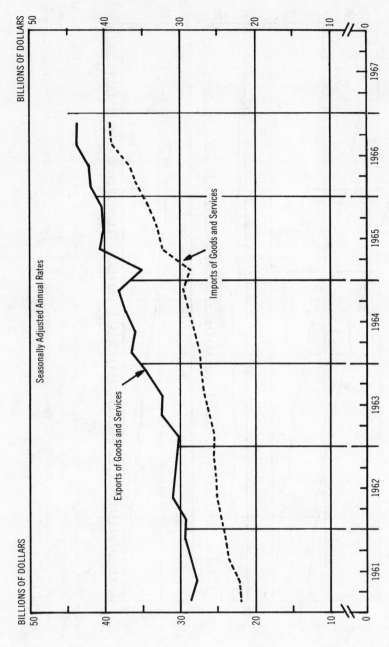

FIGURE 13–7. *Exports and imports of goods and services.* Because of their effect on the United States' balance of payments, which in turn is a "leading indicator" of business conditions, the trend of exports and imports is watched closely. When serious imbalances threaten, governmental countermeasures become likely. (From *Economic Indicators*, Council of Economic Advisers of the Joint Economic Committee of Congress, Washington, D.C.)

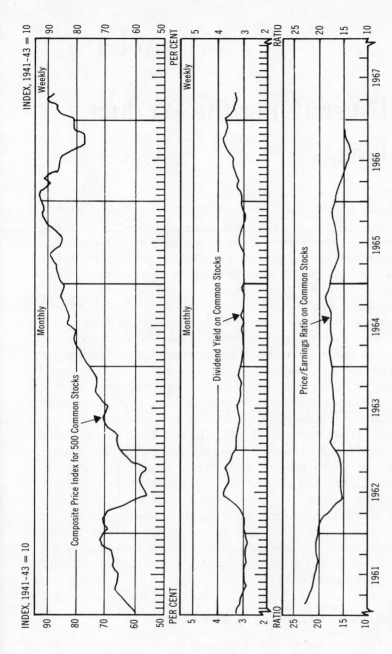

FIGURE 13–8. *Price, yield, and earnings of common stocks.* This series is particularly significant because variations in stock prices often precede other business series. In other words, stock prices represent a "leading indicator." The index is prepared by the Council of Economic Advisers from data compiled by the Standard and Poor's Corporation. (From *Economic Indicators,* Council of Economic Advisers of the Joint Economic Committee of Congress, Washington, D.C.)

CHAPTER 14

Diversifying the Product Line

Although not a forecasting problem as such, the question of what is the right degree of diversification of a firm's product line has intense forward-planning implications. In developing product lines, management must provide for enough variety to offer the selectivity needed to support a good volume of sales. At the same time, however, there should be care to avoid costly superfluity.

Anxious to meet all possible customer desires, sales people tend to push for ever widening varieties of models, designs, styles, patterns, colors, and sizes. Cost-conscious production people, on the other hand, may view this proliferation with misgivings. Only too well do they realize the toll involved in diversity that offers the customer a greater choice than he really needs—costs in additional setup times for machinery and equipment or assembly lines, in scheduling and sequencing of lots, in training operators on new items, and in other areas.

Not only production costs, but also sales and distribution expenses rise with proliferation. Tables 14–1 (p. 116) and 14–2 (p. 117) examine the major types of cost factors involved. Diversification, therefore, can be justified only to the extent that it is really needed for profitable sale of the firm's current and anticipated productive capacity. Beyond that point, variety becomes a luxury, involving either losses to the firm or unduly high consumer prices. The subject of this chapter is thus closely allied to a firm's sales-forecasting problems, since the volume anticipated will depend at least in part on the provision of adequate choices and reasonable prices.

TENDENCIES TOWARD DIVERSIFICATION

In a growing economy, many factors are at work that push toward more variegated product lines. Finding himself with sizable amounts of disposable income, the consumer exhibits a greater selectivity of tastes, preferences, and desires. Many consumers, perhaps the majority, do not seem to mind the higher price necessitated by the expanded variety they demand.

These tendencies on the part of the individual customer find their reflection in the pressures by sales people. A salesman has uncovered a new color combination, pattern, or other modification or innovation. In a short time, the news has reached the district manager and then the sales manager. "Our competitor is coming out with this; it looks like a hot item," is his argument to add something similar—the "competitive answer" to his own firm's line. Whether the item turns out as good as expected or just mediocre, there is usually no routine mechanism whereby mediocre or poor products are weeded out. There is thus a tendency for items to be added far more readily and frequently than to be weeded out. Continuing product proliferation ensues.

Occasions arise, such as during shortages of raw materials, tools, equipment, and labor, when a contraction of product lines will take place. A plant may then discover that it can maintain or increase total volume of output with less raw materials and labor input than before. A seller's market develops as shortages become accentuated. Selling is no longer a trick, and emphasis shifts to production. A production-dominated management, in turn, will continue to press for only those changes that enhance output per unit of input. Varieties and frequencies of changeovers will diminish. So long as shortages persist in the economy—usually generated by a war or other situations of stress—there is justification for a diminution of offerings for the sake of larger volume output. Tragedy may descend, however, if a production-dominated philosophy retards a return to diversity when economic conditions have begun to turn back toward growth and prosperity.

THE QUANTITATIVE APPROACH

Our predominant experience is one of economic growth and a strong tendency toward diversification of product lines. Many aspects of selling are simplified by the ability to offer a great variety and choice, but other costs will tend to rise. In resolving the issue of proper degree of diversification, quantitative methods are beginning to find useful applications. The results obtained through these analyses support but do not supplant management judgment in many crucial aspects of decision making and planning.

TABLE 14–1. PRODUCTION COSTS INVOLVED IN INCREASED
PRODUCT DIVERSIFICATION

Cost Category	Nature of Cost Increase Involved
Setups	Greater diversification means smaller lots and thus more frequent changes of dies, fixtures, jigs, and assembly lines.
Inventory	Inventories of components, parts, subassemblies, supplies, tools, and fixtures will rise to meet the increased variety of items produced.
Engineering	Product and process engineering and design will expand as products proliferate. This includes (1) design, (2) establishment of specifications and tolerances, and (3) quality-reliability test development.
Incentive System	As new items go into production, they call for proper incentive rates. Additional effort must be expended on (1) methods studies to establish work-place layouts, (2) assembly flows, (3) work standards based on time studies or methods-time measurement (MTM), (4) allowing for learning time on new jobs, and (5) supervising the system, which includes rechecks of rates and grievance procedures.
Production Control	Scheduling and control of production become more complex as the number of products, work stations, and jobs mounts. This includes (1) orderly sequencing of materials through operations, (2) balancing assembly and feeder lines, (3) evening-out work flows, (4) provision for "on-time and enough" quantities of parts, components, subassemblies, supplies, and tools, (5) availability of trained operators, and (6) the meeting of shipping and delivery deadlines.
Quality	More products and jobs going through the plant means that each item receives less detailed attention. As a result, quality will begin to drift. Rework, repairs, scrap, seconds, and spoilage will be on the upgrade. Customer complaints may rise. Hidden defects and "quality losses" will lead to a gradual tapering off of consumer demand.
Administration	General administration of a highly diversified multiproduct plant tends to become costly. The additional volumes of detail on inventory, parts in process, delivery dates, and other data coming through automated data processing all must be read, evaluated, weighed, and acted on.
Accounting	Accounting costs, such as payroll and billing, will rise concurrently with administrative expenses.

Cost Category	Nature of Cost Increase Involved
Consumer and Market Research	The more products, models, styles, patterns, designs, colors, and sizes are developed, the more difficult will it become to obtain adequate survey-sampling data to evaluate consumer preferences, to assess the general market, and to predict market behavior. Yet, it would seem to make little sense to offer the consumer or industrial customer a greater variety and selectivity without having first assured— through consumer and market research—that the expanded product line will fill a real need.
Advertising and Promotion	It is well known that the number of items shown in a single advertisement soon reaches an optimum, beyond which one may expect diminishing returns. The optimum varies with the particular products involved. Thus, increasing product diversification will call for more frequent advertising and otherwise intensified promotional activities. There is, after all, little merit in increasing the number of products offered without making the customer aware of the availability.
Selling Expense	If all of the new items are to be shown, salesmen will have to carry larger stocks of product samples. The size of the catalog will similarly fatten. Large display cases may cause a logistics problem of transport. Beyond this, the more numerous and diversified product line will keep the salesman in customers' offices for an unduly long time.
Data Processing	The numerous bits of information needed for effective management and operation of sales and marketing will increase manifold. Volume forecasts by product line, model, style, size, and design lengthen in terms of detail to be absorbed. Similarly, data on inventory available for sale, prices, discounts, back orders, and forward contracts must now be broken down for many more models and categories than was previously necessary. The sales manager, district managers, and salesmen will find it an increasing chore to keep up to date with these voluminous reports. Information that used to be kept in one's head now requires looking up. Delays may occur as bottlenecks for card punching or tape preparation arise in automated data handling.
Administration	Planning, supervision, and control of sales for the expanded product line will become more complex and costly.

ILLUSTRATIVE EXAMPLE

In order to illustrate quantitative methodology, a case history will be utilized. While various techniques are often applicable, the method of choice for this particular case is Mathematical Programing (M.P.). This technique is usually applied with the aid of a computer, and permits the evaluation of a multitude of interlocking factors in a problem, so as to discover an optimal schedule, program, arrangement, or other recommended course of action. Although the technique itself is not too complex to be understood by a nonmathematician, we will nevertheless forgo detailed explanations—relying instead on a practical example of its usage.[1]

The 8 products, *A* to *H,* of Table 14–3 represent a simplified version of the actual situation involving some 80 products or models. Rows *a* to *e* show the problem data, in terms of profit per unit (more specifically, profit contribution or variable margin), production rates in the four major production departments, and corresponding productive capacities. Considering all these data, the firm can maximize profit if it produces the program in row *f,* yielding a total profit of $64,242 per week, as shown in row *g.* As is usual when an M.P. analysis is made, products that have a high unit profit are not likely to be best to produce in large quantities, because they unduly affect production balance and would thus cause bottlenecks. It is thus that the low unit-profit item *G* should be sold in much larger quantities than *C,* with none of *A* and *B.*

The sales department, looking at the data in rows *f* and *g,* was not long in pointing it out as unrealistic from a viewpoint of marketing and sales goals. For example, it was not believed that more than 1,000 units of item *C* could be sold per week. Similar restrictions applied to all other products. The "optimum program" that had whittled down the product line to 2 items (*C* and *G*) would not be fully salable. The next step, therefore, was to perform a further M.P. analysis, this time incorporating the market limitations in row *h.* The revised optimum sales program and the resultant profits appear in rows *i* and *j.* The original program has now been reduced from 8 to 3 products (or, in the actual case history, from 80 to 30 products). We will examine this program further.

---

[1] For a nonmathematical explanation in depth, see N. L. Enrick, *Management Planning* (New York: McGraw-Hill Book Company, 1967), especially Chaps. 2 and 14.

TABLE 14-3. MATHEMATICAL PROGRAMING ANALYSIS OF A PRODUCT LINE TO ESTABLISH DIVERSIFICATION REQUIREMENTS

Analysis Steps	Salable Products								Productive Capacity, in Machine-Hours per Week	Total Profit, in Dollars per Week
	A	B	C	D	E	F	G	H		
Basic Profitability and Production Data										
a. Profit per unit, $	20	18	18	18	17	16	15	14		
b. Presswork, hr/unit	.04	.05	.04	.05	.06	.04	.06	.06	210	
c. Grinding, hr/unit	.30	.30	.30	.32	.26	.30	.22	.33	1,000	
d. Machining, hr/unit	.36	.30	.30	.30	.31	.36	.21	.36	970	
e. Finishing, hr/unit	.18	.16	.16	.18	.16	.18	.19	.18	720	
Optimum Profit Solution of Basic Data										
f. Optimum sales program, units per week	0	0	1,469	0	0	0	2,520	0		
g. Profit, $/week (= a × f)	0	0	26,442	0	0	0	37,800	0		64,242
Additional Problem Data and Revised Solution										
h. Market limitation, units/week	1,000	1,000	1,000	1,000	1,000	1,000	2,000	1,000		
i. Revised optimum sales program, units per week	0	833	1,000	0	0	0	2,000	0		
j. Revised profit, $/week (= a × i)	0	14,994	18,000	0	0	0	30,000	0		62,994

Result

Eliminate products A, D, E, F, and H from the product line. Maximum profit of $62,994 per week, attainable with available productive capacity, production rates, and unit profits, will not be affected by this reduction in the line. Aim to sell products B, C, and G in the quantities recommended in row i.

119

INTERPRETING THE RESULTS

The M.P. application to our case history provided management with highly useful information, serviceable in the diversification problem. Let us examine these findings;

1. With current production rates, productive capacity, and anticipated unit profits, an optimum sales program leading to maximum attainable profit would be as in row g of Table 14–3, or $64,242.

2. This program is not feasible because the sales department's anticipated market demand would not be adequate (row h).

3. A new program that does meet these market restrictions and would lead to an optimum is shown in row i. The resultant weekly profit, of $63,000 (rounded), is of necessity $1,250 below the earlier unrestricted maximum.

4. The new program satisfies the sales department's estimated market limitations, and it optimizes the use of our productive resources. No other program, under the conditions given above, could improve on the weekly profit shown. The program shows that 5 products can be dropped from the product line without affecting profit.

5. The new program represents a goal, not a rigid schedule guiding marketing and sales efforts.

A basic solution has been formulated, but a number of refinements were needed before the approach became practical.

REFINING THE PROGRAM

The modifications made in the product line will now be discussed in terms of the original 80-model case history.

1. After considering market limitations, the analysis yielded a reduction to 30 models.

2. This reduction seemed unduly drastic. It was found that at least 50 models would have to be offered in order to present a complete line to the trade.

3. This new requirement—for minimum volume on various products—was now added to the M.P. analysis. A new solution resulted, serving as a guide.

4. While this work (steps 1–3 above) was going on, the engineer-

ing department had been studying product designs and processing operations. Some products with high unit profits, which had been rejected by the M.P. analysis as unduly impinging on production balance and creating bottlenecks, were modified slightly. This redesign permitted procedures that eliminated bottlenecks and put these desirable products back in the running.

5. A new analysis was now performed, incorporating the new production rates resulting from the product redesign and processing modification.

6. An ultimate program of 55 models emerged, which was accepted by both sales and production.

Allocation of marketing and sales effort could now be guided accordingly.

A NEW-PRODUCTS COMMITTEE

For the future, a "new-products committee" was organized, composed of representatives from sales, engineering, and production. Its task was to (1) uncover promising new products and designs; (2) evaluate profitability, marketability, and over-all merits of these new products; and (3) test the conclusions reached by means of an M.P. analysis. Concomitantly, the committee was charged with the responsibility to review existing products for items going out of style.

ANOTHER ILLUSTRATIVE EXAMPLE

In order to emphasize the applicability of a variety of quantitative methods, we will examine another case history, taken from the production and sale of sewing thread. A seemingly small annual increase of 2 per cent in product diversification had, in the course of time, resulted in the current production of 20 types (threads of different fineness, blend composition, and twist) ; 60–70 colors per each type; and 10 forms of packaging. As a minimum, therefore, each year some $20 \times 60 \times 10 = 1,200$ separate items were being marketed. So considerable were the inventory-carrying charges that they exceeded direct-labor costs going into the product.

In order to resolve the issue of proper degree of diversification, a survey was conducted, yielding these basic facts:

1. Salesmen visit individual stores, department stores, chain stores, and mail-order houses. Usually, a visit lasts no more than 20 minutes.

2. During a visit, a salesman will have a chance to show no more than 30 items.

3. Except for decorative threads, the buyer of large stores or houses will usually leave the assortment of colors to the salesman's judgment.

4. No salesman can carry the entire selection. Instead, he will select an assortment to take on his visits.

5. Assortments among salesmen differ in detail, although they all carry a "rainbow" of colors and at least one of each type of thread.

6. Some colors are so close to each other, such as various shades of ultramarine blue, that they are difficult to distinguish. Often, the dye house has problems in producing "on shade," so that costly stripping and redyeing are required.

7. An analysis of sales among closely similar colors tended to indicate that volume was primarily a function of how many salesmen selected them. For example, for the three shades of ultramarine blue, it was found that each salesman tended to pick just one for his assortment. The annual quantity of each shade sold was approximately proportional to this selection.

When these facts had been assembled, it was decided to make a review of colors, which resulted in the rejection of "near duplications," reducing the list from 70 to 40. Next, a consumer survey yielded a further reduction of the list of colors to 30 as appropriate.

A similar study revealed that the forms of packaging could be reduced from 10 to 4. No reduction in number of types was feasible, largely because of the varying requirements of industrial users. However, it was found that some types become obsolete, and new types must be added periodically. Moreover, the firm's research and development department was assigned the task of developing threads of more universal applicability, so that ultimately there would be a reduction in number of types. In order to know what types to add and when to drop older numbers, preseason surveys among industrial users were initiated.

SUMMARY

Developing the proper degree of product diversification—enough to assure the selectivity needed for good sales volume, yet avoiding costly superfluity and redundancy—has always been a major concern of management. In a growing, prosperous, and "disposable-income society," the pressures for intensified diversification often seem overwhelming. Quantitative methods of analysis can aid management in considering pertinent factors, so as to arrive at a balanced decision.

CHAPTER 15

Evaluating a Product's Potential

Although Mathematical Programing permits a comprehensive approach to the weeding out of products that make for excessive diversification, there still remains the need to evaluate the potential of an individual product. For example, to perform a good programing analysis, we need to know, among other types of information, the maximum market potential envisioned for each item. In this chapter, we will examine various approaches concerned with the analysis of individual products and their future potentials.

PRODUCT-CLASSIFICATION SCHEMES

An individual product exists within a group of items, and it is usually identified within a scheme of classification. An example of such a system is given in Figure 15–1, but it should not be presumed that this represents a unique method. Groupings and subgroupings of products vary greatly among companies even within the same industry. Also, the level at which a separate and distinct product item is recognized will differ. For example, in many instances, color and size differences will not result in a set of distinct products; while in others, such differences will give rise to separate product identifications.

For the example at hand, with 3 product lines, 3 materials, 5 styles per material, 3 designs for most styles, 3 colors per design, and 3 sizes per color, there will result $3 \times 3 \times 5 \times 3 \times 3 \times 3$, or more than 1,200 individual product items, provided that each possible combination is made and individually identified as a product.

The proliferation of products that results from the need for variety is often depicted in the form of a tree diagram. But since it would be difficult to develop a diagram leading to 1,200 individual items, we shall content ourselves with an illustration involving only 1 line, 2 designs, 4 colors, and 3 sizes, as in Figure 15–2 (p. 126).

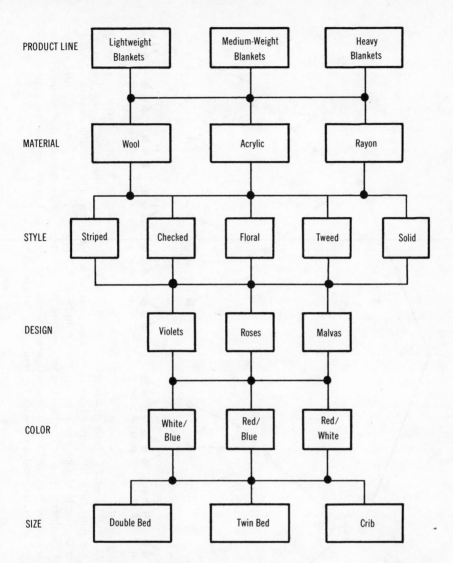

FIGURE 15–1. *A typical product-classification scheme.* The example given is for a blanket mill. In practice, groupings and designations vary among companies, usually on the basis of materials used, production processes involved, and market areas supplied.

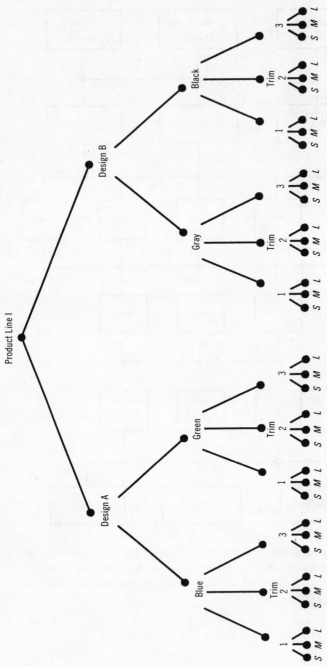

FIGURE 15-2. *Product proliferation in a product line.* With 2 designs, 2 colors per design, 3 types of trim, and 3 sizes (Small S, Medium M, and Large L), there result $2 \times 2 \times 3 \times 3 = 36$ items in this product line. If this line is regarded as typical, a company with 10 product lines would have a total of 360 items. The identification of separate "products" may be at the size level (360 products) or at the trim level (120 products). In rare instances, a firm might designate products at the design level, in this case giving a total of 20 products. Colors, trims, and sizes would then be considered merely variants of one product. In product designations, production and marketing factors pertinent to each particular firm are generally considered, with the result that definitions vary.

In evaluating individual products, it is essential that each be identified in accordance with the classification scheme. There are two reasons for this requirement. First, there are usually forecasts for various product groups by product line or other common or closely related aspects. Individual-product potentials can then be viewed in relation to the group anticipations. Second, unless there is a good identification system in use, managers and staff people may be confused on what specific product they are making evaluations or stating their judgments.

INTEGRATING MANAGEMENT JUDGMENT

Development of individual-product potentials relies to a large extent on integrated management judgment. We have seen how subjective evaluations by executives—their judgments—are aided by quantitative management-scientific analysis. In turn, these judgments play a crucial role in the formulation of problems and in the weighting of factors to be considered in the analysis. Correspondingly and significantly, management-scientific methods are also available to give structure, cohesion, and form to the process of combining and integrating the experience, knowledge, and insights provided by the individual executives' subjective evaluations. We shall examine these composite judgment-development processes with special regard to the procedures for evaluating product potentials, for which this type of approach is so essential.

EVALUATING AN INDIVIDUAL PRODUCT

When the product manager or individual sales people are asked to give their expectations with regard to the future potential of an item, it is desirable to have data on past sales experience close at hand. A form like Figure 15-3 (p. 128) will be helpful for this purpose. The information in the columns preceding "Current Year" provides the hindsight that should serve as an aid to foresight. The primarily subjective information (expectations) garnered in the column "Current Year" can be pooled, by averaging the individuals' responses. Further, a weighted average may be obtained if the judgments by certain evaluators are considered more informed than those of others.

The pooled estimates are useful as a check on the estimates obtained by extrapolating past data into the future, such as given in pre-

PRODUCT EXPERIENCE AND FORECAST

Categories Determining Value of Product	Unit of Measurement	Past Years 3	Past Years 2	Past Years 1	Current Year	Forecast Years 1	Forecast Years 2	Forecast Years 3
Price per unit	$							
Sales volume	No. of units							
Sales volume	$							
Variable margin per unit	$							
Variable margin per year	$							
Net profit per unit	$							
Net profit per year	$							
Market share	%							
Sales as percentage of firm's total volume	%							

FIGURE 15–3. *Form for forecasting sales volume, profit, and market share of a product.* Data for past years and for the current year serve as a guide to evaluating future expectations. The form is filled out by sales personnel or other qualified people. Estimates by several individuals may be pooled, usually by averaging, to obtain a composite set of expectations regarding prices, profits, and markets.

ceding parts of this book, particularly in Chapters 3 and 4. Next, discrepancies can be examined and reconciled.

RATING A NEW PRODUCT

Another type of form, which is also suitable for evaluating products in the firm's line, but which is particularly necessary when no past experience is available—the case of the new product—appears in Figure 15–4 (p. 130). The rating scale is filled out by the individual rater—the product manager, the sales manager, or sales representatives qualified by their background and experience to make valid evaluations. Weights are preassigned by the same individuals, with the provision that the sum of the weights must add up to 100 per cent (otherwise, needless complications in computations would result). Next, multiplying the percentage rating by the weights and then adding the individual results will yield an over-all product rating.

The same type of pooling, including weighted averages, as employed for the form in Figure 15–3 is applicable to the form in Figure 15–4. The over-all evaluations obtained will represent the quantitative representation of subjective "feel" about a product along a scale from "low" to "high" potential. But this subjectivity does not necessarily mean that the approach will give less useful data than one which calls for precise entries in terms of expected sales volume. It is, after all, rather difficult to obtain definitive magnitudes for a new product by executives' judgments or salesmen's opinions only. Also, we must realize that subjective ratings of a product are not used in an isolated manner. Rather, they are viewed in combination, with subsequent procedures to translate the relative positions of the subjective ratings into quantitative estimates.

CONVERTING SCALAR EVALUATIONS TO QUANTITATIVE ESTIMATES

Converting individual ratings to quantitative estimates of sales expectation can be accomplished by the methods in Figure 15–5 (p. 131). The procedures are self-explanatory. From the analysis, the less promising items, such as product 106, may be eliminated on the basis of judgment. A more objective procedure, however, would be to utilize the "high-expectation values" as effective "market limitations" in a Mathematical Programing evaluation (as previously presented).

RATING OF FUTURE POTENTIAL OF A NEW PRODUCT

Future Expectations for the Product	Rating R, Per Cent											Weight W, Per Cent	Weighted Rating W × R, Per Cent
	Low									High			
	0	10	20	30	40	50	60	70	80	90	100		
Market potential that can be realized												30	
Required amount of promotional expense												30	
Profit per unit												20	
Contribution to sales of other products												10	
Other contributions to firm's over-all program												10	
Total												100	

FIGURE 15–4. *Form for rating expectations of a new product.* This is a subjective rating scale, based on individual judgment. Weights are predetermined by a management committee. The total weighted rating represents the over-all evaluation by the individual. When several people fill out this form, the totals may be averaged (or otherwise pooled) to obtain a combined evaluation for the future expectations of the product.

CONVERSION OF RATING TO VOLUME									
Procedure	**Product Number**								**Total**
	101	*102*	*103*	*104*	*105*	*106*	*107*		
a. Rating of product, %	40	80	50	80	60	20	70		400
b. Preference ratio = $\dfrac{\text{Product Rating, \%}}{\text{Total of Ratings, \%}}$	.10	.20	.125	.20	.15	.05	.175		1.0
c. Total sales expected for next period, $									10,000
d. Product sales expected, $ = $b \times c$	1,000	2,000	1,250	2,000	1,500	500	1,750		
e. High expectation, $ = 1.20 \times d$	1,200	2,400	1,500	2,400	1,800	600	2,100		12,000

a. From the form "Rating of Future Potential of a New Product" (Figure 15-4).

b. From row *a.* For product 101, as an example, 40/400 = 0.10.

c. Extrapolation of data from past years for other, similar new products, using quantitative forecasting methods. Thus, based on an analysis of available information, the total sales volume of new products is likely to be $10,000.

d. From calculations as shown. For product 101, therefore, .10 x 10,000 = 1,000. The computations assume that the total sales volume of $10,000 will be distributed among the products in the ratio of their probable customer preferences, as formulated in row *b.*

e. Examination of past data (Figure 15-4) shows a likelihood that sales may exceed the forecast by as much as 20 per cent approximately 95 per cent of the time. Applying this 20 per cent to the forecast in row *c* gives a high expectation as shown.

FIGURE 15–5. *Form for converting rating to sales volume.* This form aids management in transforming the ratings into dollar values for expected sales volume. This procedure is primarily useful for evaluating anticipated sales of new products to be added to the product line. It may be found that some items with relatively low potential (such as product 106) are best eliminated or replaced by others.

The "high expectation" is obtained from past patterns of forecasting errors for products similar to those under current consideration. Figure 15–6 shows such a frequency distribution. From general considerations, management chooses a confidence level, usually somewhere between 90 and 97.5 per cent. In the present example, a confidence level of 95 per cent (and thus 5 per cent risk of error) is utilized. From the data on cumulative frequency, it is apparent that only 5 per cent of the time was the actual sales volume 20 per cent or higher than the forecast. This fact is further brought out by adding, under the "Per Cent" column, the values 3 per cent plus 2 per cent (equaling 5 per cent) and comparing the differences of from +20 to +30 per cent for excess of actual volume over forecast. Similarly, the "Cumulative" column reaches 95 per cent at the "Difference" level of +19.9 per cent. As another example, from the level of 11 per cent on the "Cumulative" column, we note that actual sales will be at least 15.1 per cent below forecast 11 per cent of the time.

These examples reveal the manner in which past experience can be used as a guide to forecasting future errors, assuming that past patterns in forecasting errors will tend to prevail at least in approximate degree in the future. Now, having chosen a confidence level of 95 per cent (5 per cent risk), management notes from the cumulative curve that up to about 20 per cent is the degree of excess that actual sales will exhibit over forecast at this level of probability. This figure in turn yields the multiplier 1.20, whereby the "average expected" sales in row *d* of Figure 15–5 are raised in row *e*. The allowance of 20 per cent yields the "high expectation" which will serve as the market limit for subsequent analyses (such as the Mathematical Programing evaluation).

We also note, from the fact that 4 per cent of the time actual sales fell more than 20 per cent *below* expectation, that at a confidence level of 96 per cent (100 per cent minus a 4 per cent risk) we can expect sales to be at least 20 per cent below average forecast. This determination, however, is usually less significant than that of the "high expectation." The aim, after all, is to eliminate excessive product diversification by discovering those products which even under favorable conditions are likely to earn an unsatisfactory market acceptance. Use of a "low expectation" would unduly weight the findings on the pessimistic side, aside from being inconsistent with the goals of the particular analysis.

Difference between Actual Sales Volume and Forecast, Per Cent		Frequency of Occurrence			Pattern of Frequencies, Per Cent
From	To	Number of Instances	Per Cent	Cumulative Per Cent	
-30	-25.1	2	1	1	o
-25	-20.1	4	2	3	oo
-20	-15.1	16	8	11	ooooooo
-15	-10.1	20	10	21	ooooooooo
-10	-5.1	24	12	33	ooooooooooo
-5	+4.9	42	21	54	ooooooooooooooooooooo
+5	+9.9	34	17	71	oooooooooooooooo
+10	+14.9	30	15	86	ooooooooooooooo
+15	+19.9	18	9	95	oooooooo
+20	+24.9	6	3	98	ooo
+25	+30.0	4	2	100	oo
		200	100		

FIGURE 15–6. *Pattern of past forecast errors.* For example, in 2 instances, actual sales were from 25.1 to 30 per cent below the forecast; in 6 instances, they were between 20 and 24.9 per cent higher than the forecast. Since there was a total of 200 actual instances, the 2 and the 6 become 1 and 3 per cent. The "cumulative" column, obtained by successive additions of the percentages $(1 + 2 = 3, 3 + 8 = 11,$ and so on), yields probabilities. For example, in 95 per cent of the cases, forecast errors will be 19.9 per cent or less. Therefore, only 5 per cent of the time will an actual sales volume exceed the forecast by 19.9 per cent. Similarly, only 3 per cent of the time will actual sales fall 20.1 per cent or more below the forecast. The probabilities assume that past patterns will tend to prevail in substantial measure in the future.

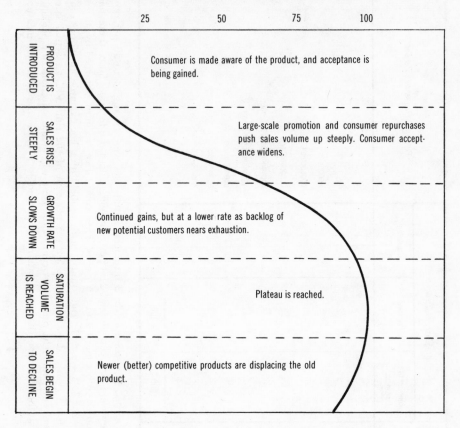

Sales Volume, Per Cent of Maximum

| | | 25 | 50 | 75 | 100 |

PRODUCT IS INTRODUCED — Consumer is made aware of the product, and acceptance is being gained.

SALES RISE STEEPLY — Large-scale promotion and consumer repurchases push sales volume up steeply. Consumer acceptance widens.

GROWTH RATE SLOWS DOWN — Continued gains, but at a lower rate as backlog of new potential customers nears exhaustion.

SATURATION VOLUME IS REACHED — Plateau is reached.

SALES BEGIN TO DECLINE — Newer (better) competitive products are displacing the old product.

FIGURE 15–7. *Principal stages in a product's life cycle.* The curve is conceptual only. Patterns of growth and eventual decline vary widely.

A PRODUCT'S LIFE CYCLE

Successive market performance, from one selling period to the next, does not represent an isolated phenomenon. Rather, it is a natural evolution in a product's life cycle, as presented in Figure 15–7. While it is unlikely that any given item will exhibit the particular pattern of growth and subsequent decline depicted here, a general trend of this nature does tend to prevail for multitudes of products in most industries.

TABLE 15–1. HIDDEN COSTS OF WEAK PRODUCTS IN A FIRM'S MARKET MIX

Cost Category	Effect
Time	Often a weak product consumes more time, proportionately, of executives, staff, and salesmen.
Price	The need for price adjustment may arise more often and more drastically than with strong products, because of the weak demand base for the product.
Inventory	Since generally low-volume items require proportionately higher safety stocks, management has a choice of either incurring this extra expense for larger inventories or else risking customer irritation from frequent stockouts.
Productivity	Low sales volume means small production lots with the resultant allocation of setup costs to these short runs. Total cost is thus disproportionately high.
Sales	Effort is diverted from the stronger, more salable, and more profitable items to support the weaker ones.
Prestige	There may be something basically wrong with the weak product—its conception, design, serviceability, or general ability to meet customer wants in its recommended usage. If one of these factors *is* the cause for weak sales, then the product is not a contributor to over-all prestige.

In recent years, a shortening of the growth phase with a concomitant increase in the rate of decline in a product's life cycle has been noted. Many subtle changes pervading the economic fabric of industrialized nations underlie this development—such as new materials, new energy sources, and new processes, as well as changing habits of work, study, and leisure-time use. It is apparent that in evaluating individual-product potentials, from one selling period to the next, we should give consideration to the typical life cycles that may be expected. Furthermore, such changes and developments in industry, the market, and the economy at large which are likely to affect or alter the life cycle must be given proper consideration. Both quantitative methods, such as are provided in this chapter, and qualitative evaluations are required for this purpose.

Shortening product life cycles also bring to the forefront the hidden costs of permitting weak products to remain in the firm's marketing mix. Such weak products are items in the declining phase of the life cycle. A compilation of the adverse effects of such products is made in Table 15–1. The table underscores the need for evaluating product potentials and for isolating and eliminating weak items from the marketing mix, while at the same time providing room for other, growing products.

SUMMARY

The methods for evaluating product potentials given in this chapter rely heavily on individual judgment. Despite this emphasis, it is possible to utilize quantitative methods in an effort to integrate these data and arrive at composite results which accurately represent total sales-volume potential. In common with all sales-forecasting techniques, the methods shown involve various risks of error and corresponding confidence levels. These factors can, however, be evaluated in terms of past experience to the extent that future patterns can be expected to work within similar interacting market forces.

CHAPTER 16

Employing the Test Market

Attainment of a good marketing mix calls for eliminating weak items while stressing new products with good growth potential. But new products cannot be added on the basis of executive judgment alone. Consumer reactions must be evaluated quantitatively, so as to yield predictive information on the basis of which the likely contribution of the new item can be estimated with an acceptable degree of reliability. For this purpose, a method of market experimentation which utilizes a *test market* has gained considerable favor. We will examine how the method works.

THE NEED FOR MARKET EXPERIMENTATION

From the conception of a new product to the consumer stage stretches a chain of questions which must be resolved satisfactorily before the item becomes a regular part of the marketing mix. Can it be produced economically enough to sell at marketable prices? Will it fit in with our current marketing channels and policies? Is sustained volume of consumer purchasing a reasonable expectation? These are but a few of the questions that arise. Moreover, they involve considerations that are not necessarily of a stationary nature. During design and development as well as during pilot-stage production, there may emerge redesigns, revisions, and modifications which reduce costs or enhance ultimate utility of the item. Under accelerated marketing, the development of promotional materials, advertising copy, and packaging proceeds simultaneously with product design and development. Time must be compressed if we are to reach the market early enough to capture a good share and enjoy a reasonable duration of product growth.

From this feverish development activity, a model may evolve that is believed to have considerable appeal. A supply of pilot quantities will be on hand. Before going into the expense of large-scale promotion and production, we should check on whether or not the consumer will like the product and, in the event of nonacceptance, what modifications of the item may be needed or desirable. The *test market,* a small geographic area which is considered representative of the nation-wide market, will serve as a laboratory in which the new product is evaluated.

Test marketing allows for experimentation with various package designs, product modifications, and other factors. Since only pilot quantities are involved, costs are relatively small. The information gained will be of tremendous value in formulating the final product version and packaging form adopted.

Test marketing represents a further time compression in the race to get to market. For example, if there are 3 possible versions of the items and 2 likely package designs, we have a total of 6 product-packaging combinations which can be checked simultaneously in 6 different testing areas.

FUNCTIONS AND FLAWS OF TEST MARKETING

Admittedly, it is difficult to find test markets that are true miniatures of the total market, but numerous localities have been found in the United States which come close to the ideal. Moreover, in the course of time, as experience is gathered in various areas, the firm can develop adjustment factors to modify local percentages of sales volume in predicting likely nationwide figures. With these limitations in mind, the functions of the test market are to serve the purposes shown in Table 16–1.

As the popularity of test marketing has spread, various complaints about its usefulness have arisen. There is, for example, the problem of "jamming," such as when a competitor knowingly or unknowingly muddies the results of a marketing experiment by offering special prices, premiums, or tie-ins on the sale of his own products. With some additional testing and relatively sophisticated statistical "filtering" techniques, the "static" created from competitive interference or other disturbances can often be mitigated—but the success of the procedures is often left in some doubt.

A further flaw in test marketing is that, after an area has been

TABLE 16–1. OPERATIONS IN A TEST MARKET

Operation	Purpose
Selection of Test Market	Utilize a restricted geographical area, which is representative of the national market, in which to test-market new products.
Projection	Observe the marketing achievements in the test area and project them nationwide. For example, if monthly volume in 2 per cent of the country is $500, then the total volume projected is $500/0.02 = $25,000.
Check of Demographic Validity	From careful review of all available data, assure that the test area is generally representative of the broad-scale market in terms of social class, age composition, and other demographic conditions.
Check of Behavioral Validity	Assure that area is representative in terms of consumption of similar or substitute products.
Check of Competitive Validity	Assure that competitive strengths in area are approximately similar to those in market as a whole. Also check that no "jamming," as a result of competitors' promotional campaigns for their products, invalidates test results.
Check of Marketing Mix	Test many factors, such as sizes, prices, promotional method, and size-price-promotion combinations.
Filtering	Use sophisticated statistical methods to filter out the effects of "jamming" and other factors affecting the validity of results.
Final Evaluation	Answer these questions: (1) Will the product sell? (2) At what probable volume rate will the product sell?

used for some time, consumers are very much aware of the fact that they "live in a laboratory" as regards their marketing behavior. This knowledge may affect their purchasing practices and general reactions toward the product. Although market researchers recognize this drawback, there seems little alternative to this type of study.

Despite the pitfalls that may attend market experimentation with the aid of test marketing, the following benefits nevertheless seem assured:

1. Even though volume predictions for a new product may turn out to be relatively inaccurate, it is highly unlikely that a poor product

will show up erroneously as a potentially good seller to add to the marketing mix.

2. When several versions of a product are tested, with different modifications, packagings, or pricings, test marketing among several areas is likely to identify the best version in the most appealing package with the most suitable price.

In the evaluation of test marketing, an analogy from production research may be of interest. When a new chemical is developed, the purity of the product and the yield of the process in the laboratory are likely to differ from the purity and yield in the pilot plant, which in turn will be differing from the ultimate large-scale production runs. Nevertheless, the laboratory data serve as a good basis in deciding on pilot production, and the results obtained give useful information regarding the decision to go into full-scale production. In marketing, as we proceed from new-product conception to consumer acceptance, we similarly seek stepwise indications to serve in the decision-making process. At all times, there should be no illusion that the data obtained provide anything more than general predictions which are subject to a considerable margin for estimating error.

FILTERING OUT MARKET PERTURBATIONS

The particular method of handling market perturbations, such as jamming, will vary with the type of problem encountered. For example, assume that a competitive promotion occurs somewhere in the middle of the 15-week test-market period. We may compute a mathematical trend line for the initial and final periods and then bridge the gap by means of a linear interpolation from the two trend lines. Instead of trend lines, long-term moving averages might be suitable.

On the other hand, assume there is deliberate jamming. Chances are that it will take the competitor at least 4 weeks to discover our test situation and develop his own competitive promotion—let us say in the form of a price cut. We can then do several things:

1. Reduce our price and note the proportional changes during the unperturbed period as against the competitor's price cut and our subsequent price cut. The percentages obtained may be used as an adjustment factor to more or less remove the effect of this jamming.

2. Start a smaller trial market in some other area and utilize the

experience in this experiment to make adjustments in the major market area.

3. Interview selected purchasers by means of random sampling, including those who bought our brand and the competitor's. From the information learned, adjustments in test-market sales data may be made to allow for the effect of jamming.

The ultimate filtering and adjustment will often involve a combination of techniques, including subjective judgment. The various factors and data collected can be further evaluated by means of multiple correlation analysis (see Chapter 7) in order to arrive at results that are relatively "purified" from jamming and other perturbation effects.

THE DECISION TO TEST-MARKET

When the chemist has developed a promising new product, management does not go into pilot production lightly. Similarly, test marketing is not undertaken without a series of studies. Usually, management must be fairly certain that a newly conceived item will have a market before there is a progression to product development, preliminary consumer checks, supplementary evaluations, and, as a final evaluation, the test market. While the detailed procedures will vary among firms, Figure 16–1 (p. 142) represents a typical approach.

It has been frequently pointed out that few products reach the development stage, even fewer experience test marketing, and only a fraction of the original candidates become items in the firm's marketing mix. The pitfalls that beset a new product on its road to market are many; for example, it may not be possible to produce the product at reasonable costs, processing facilities may not be suitable, the general "marketing package" may not allow room for it, or actual consumer acceptance may be below original anticipations. The new product must compete for a market not only on its own merits, but also in relation to other items being considered by the firm. With financial, productive, and marketing capabilities limited, only those items likely to receive greatest acceptance survive this process.

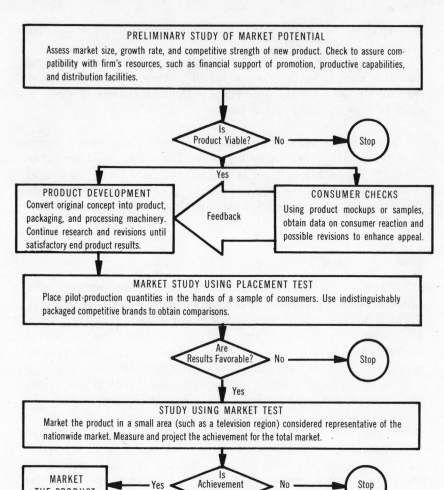

PRELIMINARY STUDY OF MARKET POTENTIAL
Assess market size, growth rate, and competitive strength of new product. Check to assure compatibility with firm's resources, such as financial support of promotion, productive capabilities, and distribution facilities.

Is Product Viable? — No → Stop

Yes

PRODUCT DEVELOPMENT
Convert original concept into product, packaging, and processing machinery. Continue research and revisions until satisfactory end product results.

Feedback

CONSUMER CHECKS
Using product mockups or samples, obtain data on consumer reaction and possible revisions to enhance appeal.

MARKET STUDY USING PLACEMENT TEST
Place pilot-production quantities in the hands of a sample of consumers. Use indistinguishably packaged competitive brands to obtain comparisons.

Are Results Favorable? — No → Stop

Yes

STUDY USING MARKET TEST
Market the product in a small area (such as a television region) considered representative of the nationwide market. Measure and project the achievement for the total market.

MARKET THE PRODUCT ← Yes — Is Achievement Good? — No → Stop

FIGURE 16–1. *New-product cycle, from conception to consumer.*

SURVEY METHODS

In lieu of test marketing, *market or consumer surveys* are often undertaken. A variety of survey strategies is available, as shown in Table 16–2. The results obtained are subjected to statistical analysis for the purpose of deriving results meaningful for marketing decision

TABLE 16–2. SURVEY METHODS FOR ANSWERING VARIOUS MARKETING QUESTIONS

| | Survey Method | | |
Question	Interview Method	Data-Gathering Instrument	Sampling Method
What percentage of households watch a certain television show?	Telephone calls	A few brief questions	Random selection from telephone directory
What additional service should a certain store provide?	Mailings	Questionnaire	Every second or third customer on file in the store
Which type of food packaging is preferred?	Personal visits	Questionnaire	Randomly selected sample of housewives

making. Since these surveys generally encompass sampling from the entire population of consumers, they usually involve more time than does test marketing. Also, it is not feasible to study reactions to several different product designs simultaneously.

A modification of these survey methods is to utilize a selected group of families—the *consumer panel*. Responses are generally solicited by mail. Brand-switching studies using Markov analysis, as discussed in Chapter 8, are based on this type of survey. Useful as these methods are, they do not fall directly within the scope of market experimentation.

INTERACTION OF MARKET FORCES

When evaluating the results of experiments and surveys, cognizance must be given to a wide variety of interacting effects of market forces. The most essential of these interacting effects are considered in Table 16–3 (p. 144). However, no systematic approach has been developed for incorporating all of these factors in the final marketing decision; thus the crucial need for experience, judgment, and circumspection in this endeavor remains.

Such quantitative data as do come from experimentation, surveys, and forecasting analyses will be of unquestionably great value to the decision maker. Usually, however, the procedures leading to this information tend to be more prolonged and complex than the executive may anticipate. There is thus often a conflict between the "practical

TABLE 16–3. NATURE OF INTERACTING MARKET FORCES

Market Force	Interaction Effect
Economic Activity	General level of business and economic activity affects attitudes in the marketplace—such as readiness to buy, interest in capital goods, and availability of credit.
Market Configuration	Impact of a firm's promotional expenditures on volume of sales depends on the level of advertising, the nature of the sales effort, and other actions and counteractions of competitors. Available marketing channels and prevailing customer and consumer preferences will contribute to a complex interacting structure, or configuration, of the market.
Creativity Factors	Originality, appeal of presentation, and placement of advertising and other promotion results in unique quality effects that can strengthen a firm's market position considerably.
Product Mix	Sales of any one product may depend on the total mix of all of the firm's products, their prices, and the market channels utilized by the firm.
Nonlinearities	Various nonlinearities will occur singly or in combination. For example, after a certain level of advertising volume has been reached, further monetary increases will yield *decreasing returns* (proportionately). As another example, until a certain *threshold level* of promotion has been reached, no results may be visible. Finally, *sales decay*, occurring when sales promotion is tapered off, is rarely linear but tends to follow a so-called *negative exponential curve*.
Over-All Conditions	Several of the forces listed above, and others, occurring concurrently and concomitantly, will produce complex interlocking and ramified market situations.

goals" sought by the executive and the attainments that can be realistically expected from market experiments and surveys or other market-research efforts. A contrast of these viewpoints is given in Table 16–4. In fact, the amount of analytical work which precedes a final marketing decision may well represent a compromise between the time and cost factors needed to arrive at valid quantitative results and the time and resources available to come to a decision. The executive, in such instances, takes a greater risk of erroneous decisions than he would if he waited for all the information to be gathered. Exigencies of the situation may well demand such risk taking.

In any event, risks of erroneous decisions are inherent in marketing decisions. While quantitative methods are available for evaluating

Goals Sought	Actual Attainments
Unequivocal Findings: "Our product will find good customer acceptance."	*Hedged Findings:* "Good customer acceptance was revealed by our sampling survey, but we were unable to study the likely response for sustained periods when other competitive brands make their appearance."
Precision: "Exactly 80 per cent of the market likes our product."	*Probability Estimates:* "It can be stated at a confidence of 90 per cent (or 10 per cent risk of error) that from 75 to 85 per cent of the market likes our product."
Simplicity: Brief statements with readily understood implications are arrived at.	*Complexity:* Lengthy findings result, with numerous qualifications and involved implications that are often difficult to fully comprehend and interpret.
Definiteness: Planning can be based on solid expectations.	*Likelihood:* Findings are subject to risks and uncertainties of the marketplace.
Promptness: "Get the answer within the next 10 days."	*Delay:* Lengthy surveys and subsequent detailed analysis will be needed to come up with usable answers.

these risks, in practice again there will usually be time limitations that call for a substitution of judgment in lieu of formal analyses.

SUMMARY

Market experimentation permits the evaluation of new products in terms of consumer appeal and sales potential. A representative segment of the total market is used as a test area in which the new product is checked. When several different designs or packagings of the new product are to be evaluated simultaneously, a number of geographically separated test markets will serve as a laboratory of consumer reactions. The ultimate marketing decision will be guided by the results obtained from these studies.

Terms Pertinent to Market and Sales Forecasting

ABC INVENTORY SYSTEM. Items are grouped by three dollar-value categories of high, medium, and low per unit at *A, B,* and *C* respectively. Decreasing concern and attention is given to the lower-valued items.

ADAPTIVE FORECASTING. Any procedure whereby original forecasts are periodically modified, based on current developments. EXPONENTIAL SMOOTHING (q.v.) is a relatively simple form of such forecasting. Instead of revising the forecast data, most adaptive methods will merely adjust certain coefficients or other factors involved in the calculation of the forecast.

ALGORITHMIC PROCEDURE. A procedure whereby all known avenues of approach are examined completely and exhaustively, and the optimum result obtained by this search is identified.

ARITHMETIC MEAN. The average of a series of items, obtained by dividing their sum by the total number of items involved. Other methods of averaging are possible, such as the *median* (middle-valued item in an array of data from lowest to highest) or the *mode* (most frequently occurring value).

BAYESIAN ANALYSIS. A statistical analysis of potential management decisions, for the purpose of determining which decision among several possible decisions is likely to minimize the risk of loss from erroneous decision making. Because of the difficulty in developing adequate data, the use of Bayesian "decision processes" is limited. Analysis procedures are complex.

BRAND-SWITCHING MODEL. An analysis of consumer propensities to buy particular brands and of the expected future effects on a firm's market shares. A MARKOV CHAIN PROCESS (q.v.) is utilized for the determination of expectations.

BUDGET. An expression of a firm's plans, in terms of the amounts of money allocated for application to various future purposes (promotion, capital expansion, and so on). A budget may incorporate expectations of income (such as from sales). See also MASTER BUDGET and SOURCES AND APPLICATIONS OF FUNDS.

BUSINESS CYCLE. Movement in business activity, which shows a wavelike pattern with alternating peaks and troughs around a trend. The interval from peak to peak or from trough to trough is the length of the cycle.

CENSUS TRACT. A selected small segment of a large population center often used for econometric, statistical, and business evaluations in instances when it is not feasible or practical to make larger surveys encompassing the entire population. The selected segment is chosen to be "typical" of the group to be studied.

COINCIDENT INDICATOR. An economic indicator that reflects current general business developments.

CONFIDENCE LEVEL. The probability that a variable will fall within certain limits. Such a level may occur with (a) forecasts and (b) evaluation of sampling survey results.

CONFIDENCE LIMITS. The range or interval within which a variable (market demand, sales, interest rates, and so on) may be expected to fall, based on a stated CONFIDENCE LEVEL (q.v.). In instances of forecasting and survey sampling, results obtained should always be associated with pertinent confidence limits.

CONSTANT DOLLARS. A series, involving dollar amounts, in which the effect of price inflation on the value of each dollar has been removed. The dollars shown are thus constant with regard to a base period, such as one year or several years in the past. The base period thus serves as the point of relative measurement, or *reference point*.

CONTROL. A management system for establishing standards (for quality, sales volume, costs) with allowable limits. In instances where actual variations exceed these limits, management's attention is directed toward the off-standard condition with a view to corrective action. The principle of "management by exception," or EXCEPTION PRINCIPLE (q.v.), is operative, since on-standard conditions are permitted to function undisturbed.

CORRELATION COEFFICIENT. A measure of relationship between two or more variables, such as the degree of sales response to advertising expenditures. A coefficient of 0.9 represents excellent correlation, while a coefficient below 0.6 usually represents negligible association among the variables studied.

CORRELATION DIAGRAM. Also called a *scatter diagram*. A graph in which the data points for a Correlation or REGRESSION ANALYSIS (q.v.) are plotted. For a two-variable correlation, there will usually be a line (computable mathematically) depicting the average relationship among the plotted points.

CRITICAL PATH. That sequence of activities in a PERT NETWORK (q.v.) which is expected to take the greatest length of time and must therefore be watched carefully if the over-all project is to be completed on schedule.

CURVILINEAR REGRESSION. A relationship between two or more variables that is best depicted by a curve or a nonlinear model.

CYCLICAL VARIATION. That variation in a time series which is ascribed to wavelike movements such as are associated with the business cycle.

DEFLATED SERIES. A series from which the effect of price inflation has been removed.

DEMAND ELASTICITY. The proportion by which an increase (or decrease) in sales volume follows a decrease (or increase) in price. If the volume change is proportionally greater than the price change, then the product is considered to have an elastic demand.

DEMAND SCHEDULE. A schedule showing the quantities of product that will be marketable at various prices. Usually, as the price increases, the quantity salable declines. Multiplication of price times quantity yields a revenue curve with a maximum point.

DEPENDENT VARIABLE. A variable that depends for its outcome on another, INDEPENDENT VARIABLE (q.v.). For example, if sales volume depends (at least in part) on advertising expenditures, then sales volume is the dependent variable. The dependent variable is also known as the *response variable* or the *output in response to a given input,* with "input" taking the place of "independent variable."

DIFFUSION INDEX. An indicator which compares the proportion of business indicators that predict a rise in business activity or a downturn of activity at a given time period.

ECONOMETRICS. The measurement of economic and related variables, using total-population or survey-sampling statistics, followed by mathematical analysis. Econometrics often builds sets of equations that serve to reflect or "model" a complex, multivariate relationship among economic and business factors.

ECONOMIC FORECAST. A forecast of anticipated economic or business conditions for specific data series or for a geographic area, a political region, a nation, or the world as a whole.

ECONOMIC INDICATOR. Any series of data that provides an indication of general economic and business conditions. See COINCIDENT INDICATOR, LAGGING INDICATOR, and LEADING INDICATOR.

ENDOGENOUS VARIABLE. A variable which is, at least in part, dependent upon other variables within a given system.

EXCEPTION PRINCIPLE. A management concept whereby only those items falling outside expected allowable limits receive detailed management attention. In sales forecasting, only those products in which actual progress does not seem to fall within the expected range of the forecast would receive attention from a viewpoint of corrective action (more promotion, revised estimate, production cutback).

EXOGENOUS VARIABLE. A variable that acts from factors and relations outside a given system.

EXPONENTIAL SMOOTHING. A method of "averaging out" and thereby smoothing the data in a time series. When extrapolated, the smoothed data become forecasts. See also SMOOTHING FACTOR.

EXTRAPOLATION. Also termed *projection.* An extension of a current trend line, curve, or other relationship. When extended into the future, the relationship thus extrapolated rests on the assumption that the set of forces operating in the past will continue to work in at least similar directions and at approximate relative strengths.

FEEDBACK. A mechanism whereby a management system, such as a forecasting procedure or actual forecast, is subject to review and revision based on experience gained with the operation of the system.

FORECAST ERROR. The difference between actually observed values and the values predicted by the forecast.

FORECAST-ERROR DISTRIBUTION. The pattern in which errors in forecasting may be distributed, which in most instances follows a normal curve.

GAME THEORY. A body of knowledge developed with regard to the problem of formulating management strategy in conflicts involving (a) intelligent opponents, such as competitors and competitive counteractions, or (b) conditions involving many elements of uncertainty, such as business activity, general market demand, weather, and the like. The latter type is also referred to as *games against nature,* in which the nature of the response is not predominantly guided by readily predictable intelligent opponents who would tend to gear their strategies toward their own optimal ends.

GROSS NATIONAL PRODUCT (GNP). Total output of goods and services of a nation, measured in terms of actual market prices, and usually estimated currently on the basis of sampling statistics.

GROWTH CURVE. A graphic representation of a company's growth in terms of sales or other measures. A growth rate is said to be "typical" if it is in the form of a slanting S—that is, slow at first, then quite rapid, and finally flattening out again.

HEURISTIC PROCEDURE. A procedure in which time and cost limitations make impossible the employment of the ALGORITHMIC PROCEDURE (q.v.). Instead, only a few approaches, likely to be quite good though not necessarily leading to an optimum, are studied. While algorithmic procedures identify the optimum, heuristic methods may serve merely to obtain a satisfactory solution. See also OPTIMIZING and SATISFICING.

INCOME ELASTICITY. The proportion by which a relative increase in sales exceeds a relative rise in consumer income. A large ratio denotes high elasticity.

INDEPENDENT VARIABLE. In a cause-and-effect system, any one or a set of independent variables will produce an outcome that is the dependent variable. For example, if retail sales are a function of shelf space allocated to a product, then shelf space is the independent, or "input," variable, and sales is the dependent or "output" or "response" variable.

INDEX NUMBER. A measure, in terms of per cent, of the change in a statistical series over time, compared to a base period. For example, if the price of a product was $10 in 1960 and is $12 in 1968, then if 1960 is the base period, the price index will be: Index Number $= 100 \times 12/10 = 120$. Many major economic and business indexes involve numerous refinements, including the weighting of various quantity factors and the combining of several series. It is apparent that the values of an index are percentages, with the base period at 100 or 100 per cent. In practice, however, there is never any reference made to the percentage term when utilizing index numbers.

INDUSTRIAL DYNAMICS. A system whereby the effects of ordering and inventory policies, from retail outlet back to the producer, are traced and analyzed. Possible improvements, through changes in ordering, inventory, or production policies on the part of the participants involved, can be demonstrated.

INDUSTRY FORECAST. A forecast of expected sales volume, inventories, prices, and other business and economic factors for an industry. An individual firm's expectations are generally tied, at least to some extent, to the forecast for the industry.

INPUT-OUTPUT ANALYSIS. A study of the amount of input of goods and services required to meet a particular final consumer demand. Interindustry effects in producing a final output must be considered for the analysis. For example, to produce more trucks, the automotive industry will need more steel; but to make this steel in larger quantities, the steel industry will also need more trucks (to transport raw materials and to deliver). Other requirements for rubber, batteries, upholstery, and the like have further interindustry repercussions.

INTERMEDIATE RANGE. In sales forecasting, this term usually denotes from 1 to 3 years. See also LONG RANGE, SECULAR TREND, and SHORT RANGE.

INTROSPECTIVE SIMULATION. SIMULATION (q.v.) using past data.

INVERSE CORRELATION. A situation where a regression line slopes downward. For example, using national income as an independent variable, it can be shown that (in many countries) birth rate tends to decline with increasing income.

IRREGULAR FLUCTUATION. Variations in a time series that represent neither trend, cyclical, nor seasonal effects. The fluctuations are generally small and of a "random" and completely unpredictable nature. The range or span within which the irregular fluctuations are likely to occur can, however, be evaluated and predicted quite well.

JURY-OF-EXECUTIVE-OPINION FORECAST. Managers of various sales regions or divisions are brought together; other senior executives and staff men join. A pooling of opinion, often including an averaging process, results in a forecast—usually for the next 6–12 months. Quantitative data may be used as aids in this jury process.

LAGGING INDICATOR. An economic series that tends to fall behind general business and economic conditions.

LEAD TIME. The time span between a decision and its consummation, such as, for example, the interval between ordering new merchandise and its receipt in stock.

LEADING INDICATOR. An economic series that tends to precede a change in over-all business conditions or in a firm's sales expectations.

LINEAR PROGRAMING. A mathematical technique for analyzing the interlocking aspects of a number of variables comprising a decision-making problem. Within the relationships and constraints imposed by the variables, an optimum solution is sought. This solution serves as an aid to management in making best use of resources to accomplish a certain aim, such as cost minimization in distribution or profit maximization in the selection of product styles to promote most strongly. The variables are generally expressed in linear-equation form. See also MATHEMATICAL PROGRAMING.

LOG CHART. A chart with logarithmic scaling. See also RATIO CHART.

LONG RANGE. In sales forecasting, this term usually denotes a period in excess of 3 years. See also INTERMEDIATE RANGE, SECULAR TREND, and SHORT RANGE.

MAD. Abbreviation for *Mean Average Deviation*.

MARKET EQUILIBRIUM. A state reached by the market as a result of brand switching, whereby eventually each brand ends up with a given (expected) market share. Because of various counteractions and unforeseen developments, a predicted market equilibrium serves as a guide only as to what would happen in the absence of efforts to avert that event. Market equilibrium in economics is considered that point at which supply and demand are in balance at a certain price.

MARKET SHARE. The proportion of a total market captured by a particular firm or product.

MARKOV CHAIN PROCESS. A system wherein the likelihood of a set of events creates an interlocking new set of probabilities of subsequent events. A Markov chain process may continue over several stages.

MASTER BUDGET. A budget comprising all aspects of budgeted expenditures such as (1) operating budget, which includes sales revenue, cost of goods sold, distribution expense, and administrative charges; (2) various nonoperating income and expense items, such as from other investments, royalties on patents, and similar factors; and (3) financial budgets, including profit-and-loss, balance sheet, depreciation schedules, receivables, and cash budgets.

MATHEMATICAL PROGRAMING. A mathematical technique for analyzing the interlocking aspects of a number of variables comprising a decision-making problem, with the objective of arriving at an optimum solution. When the variables are linear, the analysis is termed LINEAR PROGRAMING (q.v.).

MAXIMAX CRITERION. The maximum of the maximums. If, under uncertain future market demand, we choose that strategy which is most likely to maximize profits—regardless of risks of losses that are also involved—then our decision is based on the maximax principle. It is often called the "go for broke" principle, since a prudent management would not choose the maximax unless conditions were so desperate that any but the maximum gains would lead to bankruptcy.

MINIMAX CRITERION. The minimum of the maximums. For example, assume that we are faced with the problem of deciding on the size of a promotion program for a new product. The interaction between expenditures and revenues will give various profits, depending on the size of the market. Various strategies may lead to different profits depending upon market conditions that will develop. For each such condition, a particular promotion strategy will be least desirable. In retrospect, management will regret that decision most. Thus, a set of maximum regrets results. That strategy that involves the minimum of such maximum regrets is the minimax.

MODEL. A reflection, usually in terms of mathematical equations of relationship, of the interdependent and interacting activities of a real-world situation, such as the behavior of sales or prices or the response of a firm to competitive pressures. Generally, only the major variables can be considered in a model, which as a result cannot fully reflect all facets of the real-world counterpart. Verbal description may be used in lieu of, or as a supplement to, mathematical formulations.

MONTE CARLO TECHNIQUE. SIMULATION (q.v.) in which probabilistic factors are allowed for.

MOVING AVERAGE. An analysis technique for taking successive averages of data in a time series. The patterns of the time-series curve are thus smoothed. A very similar technique is EXPONENTIAL SMOOTHING (q.v.).

MULTIPLE CORRELATION. An analysis of the effect of several independent variables on one dependent variable. For example, we may study a number of factors and how they will affect sales volume, where the latter is the dependent variable. See also DEPENDENT VARIABLE and INDEPENDENT VARIABLE.

OBJECTIVE PROBABILITY. Probability estimates based on recorded past data and frequencies of relative occurrence. Inherent in objective-probability estimates is the assumption that the forces operating in the base period (on which the probabilities are founded) will continue in the future. The validity of the latter depends primarily on subjective estimates. See also SUBJECTIVE PROBABILITY.

OPERATIONS RESEARCH. The use of management-scientific methods, often with a heavy statistical-mathematical flavor, to provide a sound analysis of factors for consideration in executive decision making.

OPTIMIZING. A procedure whereby an optimum solution is sought for a problem. For example, what is the best combination of products to offer the trade for the next season? This is a problem that calls for selection of the best (or optimal) group in the right quantities. See also SATISFICING.

PANEL APPROACH TO FORECASTING. Members of related industries are called to a joint meeting, such as one sponsored by a trade association, research group, or consulting organization, to discuss needs and prospects for the coming year. A composite forecast is prepared as a result of these discussions. For example, a forecast of textile-fabric consumption may be gathered from discussions by executives of user organizations—cutters, industrial consumers, mail-order houses, chain stores, and department stores.

PARTIAL CORRELATION. In a MULTIPLE CORRELATION (q.v.), if all but one independent variable are held constant, then the CORRELATION COEFFICIENT (q.v.) for that variable with the dependent variable measures the partial correlation between these two series.

PERT NETWORK. A programed network of sequences of activities, usually laid out graphically, with time periods for expected completion of the individual activities. The term PERT is derived from Program Evaluation and Review Technique.

POPULATION. A term used to designate a large group, such as the entire region or a given market for a product, from which a sample will be surveyed. A synonymous term is *universe*.

PRESENT VALUE. The current value of an anticipated future stream of payments. For example, if money is worth 10 per cent per year (such as through investment), then $1.10 received 12 months hence is worth only $1.00 today.

PROBABILITY. A quantity between 0 and 1 or between 0 and 100 per cent, stating the relative frequency (and thus likelihood) of a certain event or outcome. Either subjective estimates or recorded experiences form the basis for probability statements, thus giving rise to SUBJECTIVE PROBABILITY (q.v.) and OBJECTIVE PROBABILITY (q.v.) respectively.

PRODUCT DIVERSIFICATION. The extent to which a company divides its product lines in terms of models, styles, and other differentiation. Excessive diversification means an undue splintering of the firm's productive and sales activities.

PROJECTION. See EXTRAPOLATION.

RANDOM SAMPLING. A method of drawing samples in such a manner that each unit or other item in a POPULATION (q.v.) has an equal chance to be selected.

RATIO CHART. A data series plotted on a graph with a logarithmic scale. On that type of scale, equal percentage increments appear in equal distances on the chart. By contrast, on ordinary scaling (arithmetic grid), unequal distances would appear. Most ratio charts are semilogarithmic, with only the vertical axis logarithmic and the horizontal (or time scale) axis being in arithmetic (or linear) increments.

REGRESSION ANALYSIS. Analysis of the relationship among two or more variables. A graph may be made for two or three variables. An equation of relationship may be made for any number of variables. When a coefficient of correlation is determined, we may refer to a regression analysis as a *correlation analysis*. The latter term generally implies that a regression analysis has also been made.

RESPONSE VARIABLE. See DEPENDENT VARIABLE.

RISK. The probability that a certain event will occur, such as that a certain class of customers will pay their bills within a given period of time. When large amounts of pertinent past data are available, and it is reasonable to assume that past factors and conditions will prevail in the future, then we may talk of *insurable risk,* which is far more definite than risks involved in UNCERTAINTY (q.v.).

S CURVE. See GROWTH CURVE.

SAFETY STOCK. A reserve quantity of products, goods, or supplies to allow for unexpectedly marked fluctuations in customer demand and for delays in delivery. Safety stock is a hedge against underestimates in sales forecasts.

SALES-FORCE COMPOSITE FORECAST. The estimates of salesmen in the field, after weighing, consideration, and review, are averaged or otherwise pooled to arrive at an estimate. This subjective approach may be combined with other methods, such as JURY-OF-EXECUTIVE-OPINION FORECAST (q.v.) and the PANEL APPROACH TO FORECASTING (q.v.).

SALES POTENTIAL. The amount of product or other goods and services that the market is likely to accept as a maximum. It is presumed that maximum sales efforts are exerted, within budgeted allowances for promotion, advertising, and selling expenses. For many firms, the sales potential is often higher than actual realization. Of necessity, sales potential is always an estimated figure. It often serves as a guide in allocating sales efforts.

SAMPLING. A procedure whereby a small number of observations is obtained from a relatively large POPULATION (q.v.). For example, to determine the interest of housewives in a new household product, a sample of 1,000 persons properly sampled may serve as an estimate. The validity of the estimate can be evaluated in terms of CONFIDENCE LIMITS (q.v.). See also CONFIDENCE LEVEL.

SAMPLING ERROR. Not a mistake in sampling, but rather the result of unavoidable "chance" or "random" fluctuations due to the "luck of the draw" in selecting a random sample. Sampling error thus refers to the fact that a sample cannot fully reflect a completely accurate and precise mirror in miniature of the population sampled. It merely represents the "best estimate."

SAMPLING UNIT. A sample usually is considered to consist of a collection of tests, observations, interviews, or other individual items. These items are the sampling units. In loose language, the term *sample* often refers to *sampling unit*.

SATISFICING. A procedure whereby, for practical reasons, it is not considered feasible (within time and cost limitations) to discover an optimum solution. Instead, a good or satisfactory solution is sought and accepted. See also OPTIMIZING.

SCATTER DIAGRAM. See CORRELATION DIAGRAM.

SEASONALLY ADJUSTED DATA. Data from which the effect of seasonal variations has been removed by means of statistical and econometric techniques.

SECULAR TREND. A long-term trend or overriding tendency of a time series, usually involving decades. See also INTERMEDIATE RANGE, LONG RANGE, and SHORT RANGE.

SHORT RANGE. In sales forecasting, this term usually denotes from 3 months to a year. See also INTERMEDIATE RANGE, LONG RANGE, and SECULAR TREND.

SIMULATION. An analysis, usually on a computer, of how a particular system, such as a marketing model (given various sales promotions, advertising expenditures, market structures, competitive actions, and counteractions), is likely to work itself out. When a simulation is applied to past data, it is for the purpose of testing its validity (assuming that future conditions will operate within a framework of past interacting forces) .

SMOOTHING FACTOR. A quantity, between 0 and 1.0, utilized in cumulatively averaging and weighting past sales volume to predict future demand. It is utilized in EXPONENTIAL SMOOTHING (q.v.) .

SOURCES AND APPLICATIONS OF FUNDS. An analysis of current and future expected sources of cash income and their expenditures for various purposes. Long-term planning depends on long-range forecasts for proper decision making. See also BUDGET and MASTER BUDGET.

STANDARD DEVIATION. A statistical measure of variability in a set of data. In a normal distribution, 68 per cent of the population may be expected to occur within a range of ±1 Standard Deviation around the population average. When standard deviations are computed for sampling data, we obtain estimates with regard to the POPULATION (q.v.) .

STANDARD ERROR OF ESTIMATE. A statistical measure of variation or "estimating error" in a regression line or other expression of regression. The word "error" does not denote "mistake," but rather factors and fluctuations which, by their nature, could not be isolated separately in the analysis and are thus lumped together as "chance," "random," or "error."

STEPWISE REGRESSION ANALYSIS. A MULTIPLE CORRELATION (q.v.) or REGRESSION ANALYSIS (q.v.) , whereby individual independent variables are examined in sequence as to their relative effect on the dependent, or response, variable.

STRATEGY. In a business context, strategy refers to the choice of a decision among various alternatives, selected by management under conditions involving uncertainty, such as the nature or degree of future demand, brand switching, competitive actions, and other factors involving risk.

STRATIFICATION. A method whereby estimates of the POPULATION (q.v.) are obtained by sampling various strata, such as geographical areas, giving due consideration to factors of proportionality among the segments.

SUBJECTIVE PROBABILITY. Probability estimates based on a person's personal evaluation of a situation, usually backed by past experience or general competence in the area. Justification for subjective probability in making business decisions or in making mathematical-statistical evaluations is usually in terms of the nonavailability of estimates of OBJECTIVE PROBABILITY (q.v.) .

SYSTEMATIC SAMPLE. A method whereby every 3rd, 5th, 10th, or 100th sampling unit, or in other words every nth unit, is sampled.

TIME SERIES. A sequence of ordered observations in terms of successive time periods and representing such data as sales volume, prices, incomes, interest rates, imports, exports, and other economic or business information.

TRACKING CONTROL. A method whereby forecasts are checked against actual performance. Differences are noted in terms of MAD (q.v.) and are cumulated for successive periods. When a tracking ratio becomes excessive, corrective action with regard to the forecasting details (such as the smoothing factors) is required. The term *tracking* refers to "keeping track" of cumulative deviations.

TRANSITION DIAGRAM. A matrix showing consumer behavior patterns in regard to brand-switching propensities.

TREND. Long-term tendency of a time series.

UNCERTAINTY. A condition inherent in all futurity. For example, whether or not business conditions at some given future date will be good, fair, or poor is largely a matter of uncertainty, even though intelligent forecasts (and "educated guesses") can be made. When large amounts of prior data are available, which are considered pertinent for the forecasts to be made, then a degree of definiteness surrounds the predictions so as to convert uncertainty into RISK (q.v.).

UNIVERSE. See POPULATION.

VARIABLE. A quantity which may vary with time or with other variables. See also DEPENDENT VARIABLE and INDEPENDENT VARIABLE.

APPENDIX

Case Problems and Assignments*

Case A: Demand Forecasting Based on Exponential Smoothing

Work-Eeze Office Machine Company

For much of the equipment sold within the metropolitan area served by the Work-Eeze Office Machine Company, there seems to be relatively minimal seasonal fluctuation in demand. Recently, the company has acquired the distributing rights within its territory of a new low-cost copying machine. From a brief review of the past 12 months of orders received, the sales manager has derived two principal conclusions:

1. There seems to be little or no seasonal variation in demand for this new equipment.
2. A continuing strong upward trend in sales volume is prevailing.

---

*Actual experience data, simplified for analysis purposes. With the exception of Cases I and Q, all names are coded and unrelated to the actual names of the firms from which the data came.

It is apparent that the copying machine is gaining increasing popularity, while at the same time shipments from the manufacturer have been arriving with longer and longer delays and generally worrisome irregularities. Even though airfreight is used, delays from 4 to 6 weeks have been experienced, and there is no prospect for easing this situation until about a year from now. At that time, the expansion of facilities at the manufacturer's plant is expected to be completed, thus relieving present backlogs and placing the supplier in a better position to fill orders promptly.

Because the company operates with rather limited capital resources, it is considered undesirable to build up large stocks. In any case, it is very doubtful whether the manufacturer would support such a large-inventory policy. Since guarantee certificates and service contracts on the equipment require the countersignature of the producer, he is able to assess the actual sales volume achieved by Work-Eeze. The producer would thus know very quickly if any of his distributors were "hoarding" his equipment for the purpose of better meeting customer demand on short notice.

The best that management of Work-Eeze can hope to do, therefore, is to order 1 month's expected requirements in advance of anticipated demand, allowing a relatively slim margin for safety stock. As an aid in this endeavor, it is necessary to forecast demand for 1 month. The technique of exponential smoothing is considered to be most appropriate for this firm's forecasting needs. Next, in order to test this assumption, it has been decided to perform a simulation study, utilizing the available sales data for the past 12 months as a basis. The following smoothing factors are to be studied by means of simulation analysis: 0.2, 0.4, 0.6, 0.8, and 0.9.

The data in Table A-1 show the year's actual demand and a few of the initial calculations, based on a smoothing factor of 0.2.

PROBLEMS

1. Complete a simulation study, utilizing these smoothing factors:
   a. 0.2 (that is, complete Table A-1).
   b. 0.4.
   c. 0.6.
   d. 0.8.
   e. 0.9.

TABLE A–1. PERIOD-TO-PERIOD DEMAND FORECAST FOR COPYING MACHINE, BASED ON EXPONENTIAL SMOOTHING, WITH A SMOOTHING FACTOR OF 0.2

a	b	c	d	e	f
Month	Actual Demand, in Units	Weighted Demand, in Units	Weighted Old Forecast, in Units	Forecast for Next Month, in Units	Amount by Which Forecast Is High (+) or Low (−), in Units
January	100	20	81*	101	—
February	90	18	81	99	+11
March	110	22	79	101	−11
April	142				−41
May	125				
June	180				
July	200				
August	191				
September	173				
October	227				
November	258				
December	244				
Total	2,040				
Average	170				

* Since the weighted old forecast = prior forecast × 0.8, where 0.8 = 1.0 − 0.2, and 0.2 is the smoothing factor, it is apparent that the prior forecast is 101 units. In particular, 101 × 0.8 = 81. Note that in this instance the forecast is also 101 for February.

2. Find the value of the mean absolute deviation (MAD) for each of the five smoothing factors. Then identify that factor which seems most appropriate, and give your reason for selecting that factor.

3. Discuss briefly what further smoothing factors, beyond those checked, might be investigated from a viewpoint of finding an even better forecast than the one obtained thus far.

4. Make a forecast of customer demand for January of the coming year.

5. Discuss briefly the validity of the sales manager's observation regarding the relative absence of seasonal fluctuation. Do the data seem to support such a conclusion?

Case B: Demand Forecasting Based on Extrapolation of Linear Trend

Work-Eeze Office Machine Company

A year has passed since completion of the simulation study (as presented in Case A). Management has now accumulated experience and data covering 2 full years of sales for the new office copying machine. The results are tabulated for review and analysis in Table B-1.

The manufacturer has requested a projection of anticipated sales, month by month, until June of next year. This information will help him plan his own production, inventory buildups, and shipping schedules, thereby providing better service to the Work-Eeze Office Machine Company. Other distributors of the manufacturer have been asked for the same type of projection.

While some of the people at Work-Eeze felt that a highly optimistic forecast should be submitted to the manufacturer, this plan was vetoed upon further consideration by all of the executives concerned. An unrealistically high forecast might indeed assure plentiful availability

TABLE B–1. MONTHLY MARKET DEMAND
FOR COPYING MACHINE

| | Demand, in Number of Units | | |
Month	Year Just Completed	Preceding Year	Both Years
January	250	100	
February	230	90	
March	285	110	
April	350	142	
May	290	125	
June	400	180	
July	446	200	
August	433	191	
September	390	173	
October	417	227	
November	614	258	
December	575	244	
Total	4,680	2,040	6,720
Average	390	170	280

of equipment against any demand that might develop. At the same time, however, Work-Eeze would lose goodwill with the manufacturer, thus jeopardizing future relations. Moreover, the manufacturer could be expected to develop his own forecasts, and if any distributor's projection deviated too markedly, the latter's forecast might simply be ignored. A reasonable and realistic projection by a distributor, on the other hand, would be likely to receive due consideration in the manufacturer's planning, inventory, and shipping schedules.

There seems to be general consensus at Work-Eeze that a simple trend line, calculated from available sales data for the past 2 years and projected for the coming 6 months, would provide a realistic forecast.

PROBLEMS

1. Calculate the equation for the trend line.
2. Extend the trend line for the next 6 months, indicating the anticipated sales volume for:

   a. January. c. March. e. May.

   b. February. d. April. f. June.
3. Plot the following:

   a. The sales volume during the past 2 years, month by month.

   b. The trend line.

   c. Projection of the trend line for the next 6 months.
4. Briefly discuss the findings.

Case C: Development of Trend Extrapolation Based on Several Years

Work-Eeze Office Machine Company

Over the years, sales of the copying machine distributed by Work-Eeze continued to exhibit a relatively good volume of growth. For the 5 years just completed, the actual rate of sales is given in Table C-1 (p. 166).

Assuming that the past trend will prevail in the future, management desires to know the expected sales volume that may be anticipated for years 6 and 7.

TABLE C–1. ANNUAL MARKET DEMAND
FOR COPYING MACHINE

a	b*	c	d	e
Years Since Machine Was Introduced	Sales, in Number of Units	Years from Central Year	Cross-Product, $b \times c$	Squared Years, $c \times c$
1	170	−2	−340	4
2	390	−1		
3	530	0		
4	660	+1		
5	750	+2		
Total	2,500			
Average	500			

* Entries in this column represent the average monthly volume for each of the 5 years.

PROBLEMS

1. Plot the sales volume for each year.

2. Compute the annual sales trend.

3. Calculate the expected sales volume for years 6 and 7 since introduction of the machine, based on the assumption that a linear trend will continue to prevail.

4. Briefly discuss your findings with particular regard to the following questions:

    a. Does a linear trend line seem to fit the actual data well?

    b. If a linear trend does not seem to fit, what other type of trend would be more appropriate in this instance?

    c. What qualitative factors, extraneous to the quantitative analysis itself, should be considered in making the final forecast?

5. Since qualitative factors are often more important than those trends which can be analyzed by quantitative means, why do we bother with quantitative analysis? Is it possible to combine qualitative and quantitative material in order to arrive at a composite forecast? Discuss briefly.

6. What are the assumptions which go into the quantitative development of trend lines, such as those prepared for Work-Eeze?

Case D: Percentage Projections of Monthly Sales

Work-Eeze Office Machine Company

Thus far, the data on sales growth accumulated for Work-Eeze have been analyzed in terms of linear trends. It is possible, however, that a curvilinear effect may be operating. An example of such a pattern, which is observed quite frequently in growth data, is the occurrence of monthly or annual increments in terms of constant percentages. In instances where such a condition exists, recognition of this factor should produce more accurate forecasts than do simple linear projections.

Management of Work-Eeze therefore wonders whether the monthly sales data (as given in Case B) might preferably be reviewed in terms of percentage growth rates.

PROBLEMS

1. Using a percentage-chart scale, prepare a month-by-month plot of sales volume for the copying machine, covering the first 2 years. On your graph, allow room to enter year 3 at a later time.

2. By means of a free-hand extrapolation line, show the expected sales volume for the first 6 months of year 3.

3. Read off the forecast, in number of units expected to be sold, for January through June.

4. Compare the new forecast obtained with that previously found (see Case B).

5. Briefly discuss the differences revealed in the comparison made (problem 4), in order to decide which forecast should be used.

6. Using a different color, enter the old linear projection on the graph prepared in problem 1.

Case E: Percentage Projections of Annual Sales

Work-Eeze Office Machine Company

A further and generally more common use of percentage projections is based on annual rather than monthly sales volume. The reason is that in all those instances where there is seasonal fluctuation in demand, an analysis of seasonal variations generally takes the place of linear- or percentage-trend studies within a year. From one year to the next, however, percentage projections may be quite applicable regardless of the pattern of fluctuations *within* a year.

Year-to-year sales volumes for Work-Eeze were previously tabulated (see Case C). It will be interesting to investigate how well a percentage trend—constant percentage rate of increase but rising absolute volume—would fit the annual sales data. In the event that percentages give a better fit, it would seem logical to make projections for the future on the basis of percentages rather than absolute values.

PROBLEMS

1. Plot the annual sales volumes on a percentage-scale graph.

2. Fit a free-hand trend and extrapolate it for 2 years. (Note that instead of a free-hand trend, a line can also be calculated. For this purpose, use logarithms of the sales-volume data.)

3. Using a different color, plot the trend line previously found for the straight-line analysis in Case C. Compare the two lines.

4. Next, make extrapolations for the lines in problems 2 and 3. Compare the differences in forecast.

5. Briefly discuss the findings from a viewpoint of their implications on forecasting of future market demand and anticipated sales volume.

Case F: Analysis of Seasonal Variation in Market Demand

Work-Eeze Office Machine Company

For the purpose of developing forecasts in the preceding cases of the Work-Eeze Office Machine Company, the analysis proceeded on the basis of the sales manager's assertion that he could discern little or no seasonal fluctuations in market demand and that he expected future years to be similarly free from this factor. In practice, however, a good analyst will have some reservations and will question, at least in his own mind, any assertions that are not based on quantitative evaluation. Certainly, one should not blindly accept such a statement of opinion as a fact, even when it is a strong opinion. The analyst should:

1. Receive and acknowledge the information submitted to him, to the effect that from a consideration of experience and general impressions it appears that seasonal fluctuations are likely to be absent or negligible.

2. Subject the information received to a test. For example, the data on actual sales volume, provided with Case B, can be subjected to a study in order to detect any seasonal variation that may be present.

3. If the data analyzed do show indications of seasonal variations, present this fact. The purpose here will be to seek agreement on the facts and to provide for future allowance for seasonal fluctuations in the analysis and forecasts.

It should be realized that step 3 may cause some upsets of pet theories, and thus much patience will be needed in first making sure of one's ground, then properly documenting one's findings with all pertinent quantitative and qualitative data that can be marshaled, and finally presenting the results and winning agreement.

PROBLEMS

1. Review the monthly sales data for the 2 years (Case B) for evidence of seasonal variation.

2. Plot the results of your analysis.

3. Prepare a brief summary of your findings, which will be submitted to management.

Case G: Control Limits for Seasonal Variation in Sales Volume

Work-Eeze Office Machine Company

For the purpose of this case, the following assumptions will be made:

1. Management has accepted the view that, contrary to earlier expectations, a seasonal factor does seem to be operating in the market for the new copying machine.

2. During the entire second year since introduction of the new machine, sales have averaged 390 units per month.

3. A forecast of 600 units per month has been made for the coming year.

4. During the first 4 months of year 3, monthly sales volumes were as follows:

Month	Sales, No. of Units
January	580
February	500
March	540
April	600

Management desires to utilize a control-chart approach, whereby sales are charted from month to month. When there develops an indication of an error in the original forecast, revision in sales anticipation is desirable. As an example of such corrective adjustments, actual sales falling below the lower control limit may signify (1) inadequate selling effort or (2) lower future market demand than originally expected.

Large sales volume, with the month-to-month trend of actual sales falling beyond the upper control limit, usually call for upward revision of sales anticipations and corresponding increases in (1) ordering stock or (2) building up inventory.

PROBLEMS

1. Plot the past seasonal patterns against the sales volume anticipated for year 3.

2. Add control limits at a confidence level of 90 per cent.

3. Repeat problems 1 and 2, but this time utilize control limits at the following confidence levels in per cent:
   a. 95.
   b. 80.
   c. 70.
   d. 50.

4. Plot the actual sales for the first 4 months of year 3 on the chart you have prepared.

5. Briefly report your findings to management, based on the work in problems 1, 2, and 4.

6. If you also completed part or all of problem 3, prepare a report based on the additional findings obtained.

Case H: Trend of Sales Volume versus Advertising Expenditures

Fashionable Loom Creations, Inc.

Fashionable Loom Creations, Inc., is in the business of weaving and finishing fine worsted fabrics that appeal to the better-quality women's wear trade. Generally, the firm purchases regular and novelty yarns from various spinning mills, both domestic and foreign, for use in highly fashionable fabric designs. The processing operations of winding the yarn, twisting it, placing it on large beams, and then weaving and finishing the fabric are performed with a high degree of workmanship and under rigid quality controls at the two plants owned by the firm.

New fabric designs are required for each of the two annual seasons, spring and fall. Under normal conditions, the sales volume for the spring season is approximately the same as that for the fall. Recently, however, a continuing decline in the sale of sportswear fabrics has been experienced. Management is particularly concerned over this situation, since the losses in volume have occurred despite increasing expenditures for advertising and selling promotion.

The nature of the losses, during the past 2½ years, are docu-

Season Number *	Sales Volume, $1,000	Promotion Expenses, $1,000	Publicity-Exposure Index †
1	90	12	70
2	70	15	60
3	75	16	50
4	60	14	30
5	55	18	40
Total	350	75	250
Average	70	15	50

* Season 5 is the one just completed. Season 1 is the earliest considered for the analysis.

† Publicity exposure is measured in terms of a specially prepared index, developed by the marketing manager, giving weight to these factors: (1) number of articles appearing in the trade and consumer press referring to the firm's fabrics, (2) length of text, (3) number and size of fabric design reproductions published with each article, and (4) circulation reached by each medium. A high index figure indicates a large degree of publicity exposure.

mented in Table H-1. The table shows the spring and fall of one year, the spring and fall of the next year, and the spring just completed.

PROBLEMS

1. Plot the sales volume against the following:
   a. Time (that is, seasons).
   b. Promotional expense.
   c. Publicity exposure index.
2. Calculate and draw trend lines for the data plotted in problem 1.
3. You will note some apparently paradoxical results. Discuss possible reasons for these observations, first in general terms and then with regard to the particular problems faced by the management of this firm.

Case I: Simulation of Order and Merchandise Flows

Institute for Applied Technology

In recent years, the Institute for Applied Technology of the National Bureau of Standards has engaged in studies of industrial and business processes by means of simulation models. As the Institute explains:

> Industrial models are something like the wind-tunnel models used by the aircraft industry . . . to predict the in-flight behavior of an airplane design before the plane is actually built . . . thereby maximizing the probability that the ultimate design will be successful.

> These early physical models led to newer kinds, where the tunnel could be replaced by a computer which calculated what would happen in the wind-tunnel. It is called a *simulation model* because it simulates real physical conditions through the use of equations describing those conditions.

> There are obvious advantages to an industry or company if its own performance can be studied, analyzed and predicted in the same way. New policies can be tested out before being put into practice. Studies of the structure of an existing industry might suggest solutions to long-term problems of that industry.

Some of the questions that might be answered by such simulation studies are the following:

1. What effect will increased investment in new technology have?
2. Where might such investments best be made?
3. How would shifts in market demand affect an industry?
4. Is there a way, through better information flows, to improve coordination of sales, inventories, and production?

Identification of new markets, improvement of existing ones, and generally more successful operations, based on the findings of simulation studies, have occurred in some industries. The following is a simplified illustration, developed by the Institute for Applied Technology, to demonstrate the application of simulation.

THE INDUSTRY STRUCTURE

The simplified industry consists of a factory, a wholesaler, and a retailer, who are manufacturing "widgets." Consumption of widgets has averaged 10 a week for years, with a cyclical high of 12 and a low of 8 in retail sales. But the widget cycle is only a symptom, not the cause, of existing industry problems. The cause may be the way the industry interprets demand, the manner in which it makes operating decisions, or the inability of widget-producing machines to adjust output quickly to real market demand.

In order to check further into these questions, a research team is chosen to study the industry. As a first step, retailers, wholesalers, and factories are visited. Questions are asked on how orders are processed, how production rates are determined, and how inventories are kept, among other operating policies. Here is what the interviewers learn:

Retailer. The typical retailer says he usually keeps an inventory of 10 widgets. At the end of each week, he notes what he has sold and orders a like amount from the wholesaler. It takes 3 weeks for the goods to arrive, but since he orders weekly he receives a shipment weekly. "Funny thing is," he says, "since I order exactly what I sell, you'd think I'd have an inventory of 10 widgets all the time. But sometimes I'm nearly out of stock, and other times I've got widgets coming out of my ears."

Wholesaler. The wholesaler also tries to keep an inventory of 10 widgets. When he receives an order, he fills it from inventory. Once a week he totals his orders and orders a like amount from the factory. "It takes me 3 weeks to get widgets from the factory. I try to order regularly, so I'll have enough on hand," he says; "but I can never seem to match demand and inventory. Yet my orders and shipments are based on only the real demand I see."

Factory Manager. When the factory manager receives an order, he requires about 1 week to process and ship it. When he sends out widgets, he also orders his production line to start a like amount for inventory. "But," he says, "it takes a week to set up the equipment and get the widgets produced and into stock."

THE INDUSTRY MODEL

From this type of information and further investigations, the research team can now draw a diagram of the industry and its operation, as shown in Figure I-1. This diagram represents the industry "model." The relationships depicted could readily be transformed into an equation type of model.

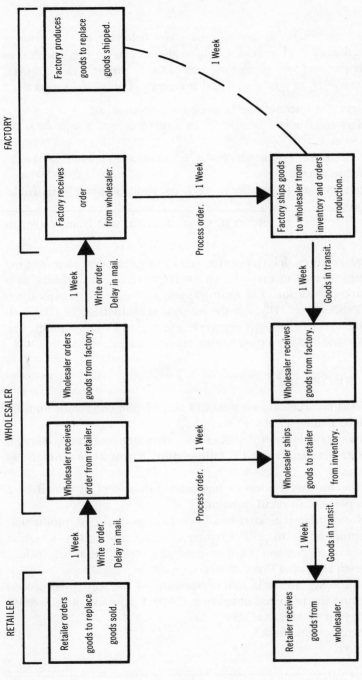

FIGURE I-1. *Flow of orders and goods in widget industry.* The structure of the industry and the time relations between retailer, wholesaler, and factory are depicted, as related to the flow of orders, the accumulation of inventories, and the shipment of goods.

SIMULATION

The research team now simulates the behavior of the industry over a typical 15-week period. Utilizing the model, we begin with consumer demand at any given time and trace it through the industry, noting its effects on production and inventory. The model shows that:

Orders sent from retailer in week 1 = sales demand.

Orders received by wholesaler in week 2 = orders sent from retailer in week 1.

Goods shipped from wholesaler in week 3 = orders received by wholesaler in week 2.

Goods received by retailer in week 4 = goods shipped from wholesaler in week 3.

Goods received by retailer in week 4 = orders sent from retailer in week 1.

The structures, delays, policies, and other behavioral factors of the industry permit us to map the entire response of the industry to a given market condition. The results appear in Figure I-2, based on the data in Table I-1 (p. 178) . For the purpose of tabulating, we start with a typical demand of 10 units per week, which rises to 12, gradually levels off to a low of 8, and then begins upward again.

PROBLEMS

1. Calculate the data for weeks 14 and 15, and enter your findings to complete Table I-1.

2. The way the industry operates, what happens to production and inventory when demand is falling? Why is this a paradoxical development?

3. How much variation in inventory, in per cent, is caused by a rise of 20 per cent in retail demand?

4. Noting that, long after retail demand has stabilized, production and inventory levels are still changing and that production is highest at the time retail demand is lowest (and vice versa) , what conclusions do you reach regarding this industry?

5. Supposing you felt that a speedup of the ordering process would reduce the problems noted in problem 4, how specifically would you check your ideas for validity?

6. Perform this check.

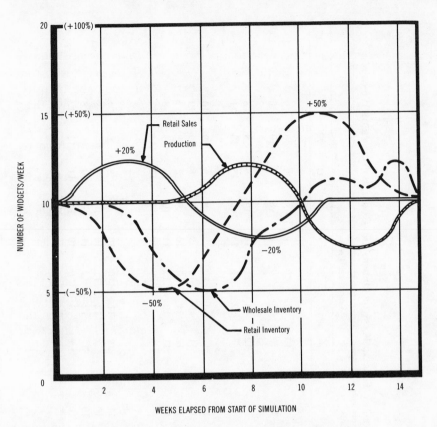

FIGURE I-2. *Simulation results in widget industry.*

7. One of the structural relationships of the model, in words, is: "Since on the average it takes 2 weeks to prepare, mail, and ship the retailer's order, the wholesaler's shipment to the retailer this week will equal the retailer's orders of 2 weeks ago."

In symbols, if WS = Wholesale Shipment, RO = Retail Order, and subscript t = Time now, then:

$$WS_t = RO_{t-2}$$

Prepare similar equations of the model discussed under the heading "Simulation" in this case.

TABLE I-1. SIMULATION RESULTS OBTAINED BY TRACING FLOW OF ORDERS AND GOODS, IN NUMBER OF WIDGETS

Activities	Successive Weeks														
	1	2	3	4	5	6	7	8	9	10	11	12	13	14	15
Retailer															
Average sales	10	11	12	12	11	10	10	9	8	8	9	10	10	10	10
Order sent to wholesaler	10	11	12	12	11	10	10	9	8	8	9	10	10	10	10
Goods received from wholesaler	10	10	10	10	11	12	12	11	10	10	9	8	8		
Inventory level	10	9	7	5	5	7	9	11	13	15	15	13	11		
Wholesaler															
Order received from retailer	10	10	11	12	12	11	10	10	9	8	8	9	10		
Order sent to factory	10	10	11	12	12	11	10	10	9	8	8	9	10		
Goods sent to retailer	10	10	10	11	12	12	11	10	10	9	8	8	9		
Goods received from factory	10	10	10	10	10	11	12	12	11	10	10	9	8		
Inventory level	10	10	10	9	7	6	7	9	10	11	13	14	13		
Factory															
Order received from wholesaler	10	10	10	11	12	12	11	10	10	9	8	8	9		
Goods sent to wholesaler	10	10	10	10	11	12	12	11	10	10	9	8	8		
Goods produced	10	10	10	10	10	11	12	12	11	10	10	9	8		
Inventory level	10	10	10	10	9	8	8	9	10	10	11	12	12		

Case J: Multiple Correlation Analysis

Fashionable Loom Creations, Inc.

During a study of the causes of the recent persistent downward trend in the sales volume of the firm's sportswear fabrics, the company controller has obtained the following information from a review of available records and data, as well as from discussions with the sales, marketing, quality-control, and industrial engineering departments:

1. Although there has been a decline, industrywide, of some 5 per cent in market demand from season to season, this relatively small general downward trend in the sportswear-fabric field cannot explain the far more serious decline of the firm's sales.

2. The firm seems to be rapidly losing its market share of sportswear fabrics.

3. There seems to have been no deterioration in the quality of the yarns purchased, the dyes used, or the workmanship in weaving, finishing, and other processing operations.

4. Neither the salesmen nor the customers interviewed in a sampling survey felt that there has been a lack of creativity, novelty, taste, or general appeal in the patterns, designs, and colors offered by the company.

5. Costs and prices of the fabrics remain in line with competition.

After further investigation, the controller has found that two of the leading trade publications have been giving markedly less editorial space to the firm's sportswear fabrics. A similar tapering off of editorial coverage has also been noted in the consumer fashion magazines. He feels that a large part of the blame for this development has to be laid to the promotion department, which lost a key writer of publicity releases. The new man assigned to sportswear coverage does not seem to produce effective copy, from a viewpoint of interesting and attractive text or well-chosen photographs and related illustrative material.

The controller feels that with a proper analysis, the data previously shown in Case H, could be utilized to support his findings.

PROBLEMS

1. Using the techniques of multiple correlation analysis, develop an estimating equation showing the relative effect on the sales of the firm's sportswear fabrics of:

    a. Promotional expense.

    b. Publicity exposure.

2. If an electronic computer is available, extend the multiple correlation analysis to include also the effect of time over the 5 seasons.

3. In what manner does the analysis performed in problem 1 support the controller's conclusions?

4. What further information is provided by the analysis in problem 2? (Answer only if you performed the work called for in that problem.)

5. What insights does the multiple correlation analysis provide for management? Point out why these insights could not be gained without multiple correlation analysis.

6. Discuss the steps management might take to reverse current trends.

Case K: Determining Proper Degree of Diversification

Homeglow Table Lamp Manufacturers

For several years, disagreement has existed between the sales and the production department concerning the desirable degree of product diversification. Sales people have felt that only with a large variety of offerings is there a reasonable chance of meeting the challenge of competition and enlarging the firm's market shares. Production management, on the other hand, has pointed to the additional costs incurred for a large variety of setups, blanking and forging dies, and parts inventories. In turn, with sales calling for competitive pricing in the face of these relatively high costs, a growing "profit squeeze" has developed.

For the future, top management wonders whether it might not be preferable to reduce the product line by offering fewer styles, but to en-

TABLE K–1. MARKET SHARE, ADVERTISING EXPENDITURES, AND PRODUCT DIVERSIFICATION OF LAMP MANUFACTURER*

	Firm's Market Share, Per Cent	Advertising Expenditures, in $1,000	Product Diversification, in Number of Styles
	3	60	18
	4	70	16
	6	100	20
	5	130	22
	5	100	18
	7	140	26
Total	30	600	120
Average	5	100	20

* The data represent 6 seasons. Seasonal factors and trend are not considered important, because the data are given in relative terms, as a percentage of the total market.

gage in more vigorous advertising and related activities. In order to arrive at a definite decision, it is felt desirable to review past experience data. The following data (shown in Table K-1) are available for the past 6 selling seasons: (1) actual sales expressed as the firm's share of the total market, (2) expenditures on advertising, and (3) product diversification in terms of number of styles offered.

From this information, it is believed possible to develop a procedure that will document the relative effect of advertising expenditures and product diversification, each analyzed for its distinct bearing on the firm's market share.

PROBLEMS

1. Formulate a quantitative procedure that evaluates the relative effects on sales of:
    a. Advertising expenditures.
    b. Product diversification.
2. Express the results in equation form.
3. Discuss the findings and their implications.

Case L: Sales Forecasting with Multiple Correlation Analysis

Superior Supply Company

From past experience, management of the Superior Supply Company is well aware of the importance of new-housing starts and foreign imports on its sales volume. Data for the past 8 years are given in Table L-1.

Management desires an equation expressing the effect of new-housing starts (within the area served by the company) and of imports of competitive products on the company's sales volume. Also, it is anticipated that in the coming year, the number of new-housing starts will be 30,000, while foreign imports of competitive products will be $30 million.

TABLE L–1. SALES VOLUME RELATED TO NEW-HOUSING STARTS
AND FOREIGN IMPORTS FOR A SUPPLY COMPANY

Year	Firm's Sales, in $1 Million	New-Housing Starts in Area Served, 1,000's of Houses	Foreign Imports of Competitive Products, in $10 Million
1	7	19	0.9
2	3	15	2.0
3	6	30	1.9
4	9	25	1.5
5	2	10	2.5
6	4	20	2.0
7	3	15	2.8
8	6	26	2.4
Total	40	160	16.0
Average	5	20	2.0

PROBLEMS

1. Develop the equation desired by management and make such further comments as will be appropriate.

2. Supply a specific forecast of sales expectations for the coming year.

Case M: Predicting Market Shares as Basis of Marketing Strategy

Textmaster Technical Publications

Organized for the purpose of developing superior-quality texts for technical schools, Textmaster has expended considerable sums to promote new basic texts in mechanical, electronics, and industrial engineering. As a result of journal advertising, mail circulation, liberal distribution of examination copies, and regular sales visits to teachers, the texts rapidly gained adoptions in 40 per cent of the courses taught in the country. The largest single competitor has gained 20 per cent of this market, while all others combined hold the remaining 40 per cent.

With the use of a carefully designed reporting form, which was filled out by salesmen after each visit, a basic pattern of loyalties and switches in textbook adoptions was discernible among the teachers. In fact, a computer analysis based on the salesmen's reports revealed the transition matrix shown in Table M-1.

TABLE M–1. EVALUATION OF MARKET SHARE IN SECOND PERIOD
FOR A TECHNICAL-BOOK PUBLISHER

Textbook Bought in Initial Term*	Percentage of Teachers Remaining Loyal or Switching during Second Term		
	Textmaster Book	Closest Competitor's Book	Other Competitor's Book
Textmaster book	50 loyal	20	30
Closest competitor's book	30	50 loyal	20
Other competitor's book	10	10	80 loyal

* *Term* refers to a school term, quarter, semester, or other similar period. For example, in 50 per cent of the courses where a Textmaster book was used in the initial term, it was readopted in the second term. In 20 per cent of the courses, however, the closest competitor's text was substituted; while in the remaining 30 per cent, some other competitor's title was chosen to replace Textmaster's book.

Top management is satisfied that 40 per cent represents the share of the market it desires. Consequently, it is now proposed to go into a new area: the development and promotion of texts in the data-processing field. Both manpower and financial resources now devoted to mechanical, electronics, and industrial engineering would have to be reallocated to data processing.

While these discussions were going on among the executives, one of the market-research analysts prepared a Markov study for the current market shares and transition matrix. From this study he has made these significant predictions:

1. If the firm continues its past promotional efforts in undiminished magnitude and if competitors do not increase their efforts, it may be anticipated that Textmaster sales will slide.

2. In fact, current trends are such that—with continued, heavy marketing effort on the firm's part—Textmaster's sales of technical books will slide to 30 per cent in the next period (representing the 3–4 months of a school quarter, term, or semester) and eventually to a low of 23 per cent.

3. Furthermore, if the company slackens its efforts and its competitors increase their promotion, Textmaster's market share will drop to less than 23 per cent.

The research analyst submitted his Markov analysis to support the first two points. No precise data could be given for the third point, since no estimate had yet been made of the increased effort that might be expended by competitors. The results of the analysis are nevertheless sufficient to show the need for considerable caution with regard to any reallocation of funds.

PROBLEMS

1. Evaluate new market shares for buying periods 2 through 5.
2. Calculate the shares during market equilibrium.
3. In what manner do the data of problems 1 and 2 support the conclusions reached by the market-research analyst?

Case N: Sales Promotion under Uncertainty

Excelsior Corporation

Sales of a newly developed line of consumer products, recently mar-keted by Excelsior, are lagging badly. In order to boost sales, 3 alterna-tive promotional programs have been developed. The pertinent data are given in Table N-1.

The probabilities of adequacy of promotional programs and of oc-currence of a good, fair, or poor year of general economic and business conditions are based on executive opinions, supported by a brief sur-vey and by published forecasts for the economy.

Profits were estimated by means of (1) sales-volume estimates, (2) profits-per-unit calculations, and (3) anticipated costs of promotional programs.

Management wonders which program will be likely to yield the highest expected profit.

TABLE N–1. ALTERNATIVE PROMOTIONAL PROGRAMS
AND THEIR RESULTS

		General Economic Conditions		
	Probability of Adequate Response, Per Cent	*Good*	*Fair*	*Poor*
		Probability of Occurrence, Per Cent		
Program		*10*	*30*	*60*
		Profits in $100,000 per Year		
Intense	50	2.0	1.5	0.5
Medium	30	1.8	1.3	0.3
Minimal	20	1.0	0.5	−0.5

PROBLEMS

1. Represent the problem in the form of a tree diagram.
2. Evaluate the expected profits, based on the problem data.
3. Identify the program which is likely to yield the highest ex-pected profit.
4. What is the magnitude of this profit?

Case O: Decision Making under Uncertainty

Sheeralon Corporation

Sheeralon Corporation is a chemico-textile concern, currently considering the proper size for a plant to produce its new fiber, "Sheerstrand." Whether a small, medium, or large facility is to be erected depends upon the degree of market penetration that may be expected to prevail.

CASH POSITION

Using data supplied by market-research estimates and cost accounting, a computer simulation study[1] has been performed, yielding the data shown in Table O-1 regarding profitability. The specific evaluation criterion used was the net cash position expected 10 years after the date of plant completion. Net cash is defined as cumulative net earnings plus reserves for depreciation minus permanent investment and working capital.

TABLE O–1. EXPECTED CASH POSITION IN YEAR 10
OF OPERATION, IN MILLIONS OF DOLLARS

	Rate of Market Penetration		
Plant Size	High	Medium	Low
Small	50	30	20
Medium	70	60	10
Large	90	40	−10 (loss)

RATE OF MARKET PENETRATION

A poll of executives in the company has revealed that opinions vary regarding the rate of market penetration to be expected. Execu-

---

[1] For details on the nature of such a study, see Sigurd L. Andersen's contribution in N. L. Enrick, *Management Operations Research* (New York: Holt, Rinehart and Winston, 1965), Chap. 21.

TABLE O-2. EXPECTED RATE OF MARKET PENETRATION

Rate of Market Penetration	Executives Stating Opinions	
	Number	Per Cent
High	10	50
Medium	4	20
Low	6	30

tives polled included district sales managers, the manager and vice president of sales, the controller, and other vice presidents. The results obtained are shown in Table O-2.

PROBLEMS

1. Analyze the data presented and identify the strategy likely to yield the best expected net cash position in year 10 of operation. In particular:
   a. Prepare a tree diagram of the problem.
   b. Evaluate the expected profits, based on the information provided.
   c. Specify which plant size is likely to yield the highest (expected) cash position in year 10 of operation.
   d. Specify the expected cash position corresponding to the recommended plant size.

2. Discuss what further information, not explicitly given above, would be of value in this decision-making problem. Why is it generally impossible to work with more than estimates, guesstimates, and similar "uncertainties" with regard to the crucial factors in the analysis?

Case P: Competitive Bidding under Uncertainty

Blackstone Construction Company

Invitations to bid on the construction of a large shopping center have been received at company headquarters. Calculations by architects, engineers, and accountants show that construction costs are likely to vary according to the weather conditions prevailing during the time of outdoor building in late summer, fall, and early winter. Consequently, the weatherman was consulted in preparing part of the data shown in Table P-1.

Management is considering three types of bids, which we may label "high," "medium," and "low" at $15, $14, and $13 million. A high bid, it is felt, has only a 10 per cent chance of acceptance; while a medium bid stands a 20 per cent chance. For a low bid, there seems to be a 70 per cent likelihood of acceptance. Management is anxious to obtain this job because idle equipment and men will cost about $100,000, and there is only a 60 per cent chance that another contract will come along to take up the slack if the present opportunity is lost.

TABLE P-1. WEATHER CONDITIONS RELATED
TO CONSTRUCTION COSTS

Weather Condition	Likelihood of Condition Prevailing, Per Cent	Construction Costs, in $1 Million
Mostly sunny	20	12
Much rain	20	14
Mixed	60	13

PROBLEM

Evaluate Blackstone's situation and make a recommendation to management that will maximize "expected value."

Case Q: Product-Line Diversification

International Telephone and Telegraph Corporation

Following the introduction of the company's "Selectrocrown Portable Cord Self-Specification Guide" in chart form (Fig. Q-1, p. 190), the manager of advertising and sales promotion explained:

The basic problem has been that many users just bought a specific type of cord, when perhaps a lower-priced one would have done. This is graphically portrayed on the chart. The Royal EZC 4-crown is the best for resistance to oil, abrasion, and other characteristics, but not every application requires this. The 4-crown costs more, and therefore if a 1-, 2-, or 3-crown would do the job, a lot of money can be saved.

The crown system of identification was developed both from a practical and a promotional viewpoint.

Instructions for the self-specification guide are as follows: "Use left-hand column to select those properties which are required for your application. Then pick the insulation which rates the highest in these properties. If more than one classification is suitable, select the insulation with the least number of crowns."

It is apparent that this system avoids unnecessary overdiversification, thereby saving production, inventory, and administrative costs for both supplier and user.

PROBLEMS

1. What steps would seem needed to develop a practical program resulting in a product line that avoids overdiversification and yet meets customer requirements? Outline the steps of such a program, supplementing these with a flow chart.

2. Discuss in detail how savings in production, inventory, and administrative costs accrue to both supplier and user.

3. In what manner is the development of the Selectrocrown system different from marketing trends observed in many other industries?

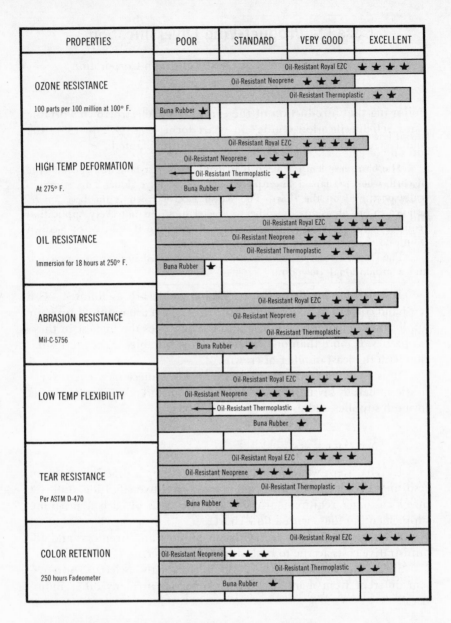

FIGURE Q–1. *Product-selection guide.* The company's four portable cords are identified by properties, quality ratings (from "poor" to "excellent"), and relative price (from 1 crown = lowest to 4 crowns = highest).

Case R: Forecasting Based on Product Performance Data

Reliable Standby Equipment Company

Reliable Standby Equipment Company is engaged in the production and sale of emergency-power sources. The line includes portable units as well as larger equipment and a variety of automatic switchover devices that operate in the event of a power failure.

For one of these products, a form entitled "Product Experience and Forecast" (Fig. R-1, p. 192) has been partly filled. The data represent past accounting and sales records and forecasts by qualified persons in the sales and marketing areas of the firm.

PROBLEM

Using the information provided in the form in Figure R-1, complete the missing calculations for sales volume in dollars per year, variable margin per year, and net profit per year.

Case S: Evaluating the Potential of a New Product

Precision Instrumentations, Inc.

As a by-product of aerospace research in another division of Precision Instrumentations, the manufacturing division of the firm has been offered a new laboratory instrument. The market is not considered large enough to permit extensive research.

In order to evaluate the potential of the new instrument, prior to a decision on actual marketing, the sales manager has asked various people in the firm who are in a position to have some knowledge and judgment on the situation to rate the product. A typical form is shown in Figures S-1 (p. 193).

PROBLEM

Complete the rating form and obtain a total weighted rating for the product.

PRODUCT EXPERIENCE AND FORECAST

Categories Determining Value of Product	Unit of Measurement	Past Years			Current Year	Forecast Years		
		3	2	1		1	2	3
Price per unit	$	100	120	150	160	180	200	220
Sales volume	No. of units	500	600	400	600	700	900	1,100
Sales volume	$							
Variable margin per unit	$	10	20	25	25	30	30	30
Variable margin per year	$							
Net profit per unit	$	5	10	10	10	15	15	15
Net profit per year	$							
Market share	%	5	5	3	5	6	7	8
Sales as percentage of firm's total volume	%	6	6	5	4	3	2	2

FIGURE R-1. *Form for forecasting sales volume, profit, and market share of an emergency-power device.*

RATING OF FUTURE POTENTIAL OF A NEW PRODUCT

Future Expectations for the Product	Rating R, Per Cent												Weight W, Per Cent	Weighted Rating $W \times R$, Per Cent
	Low										High			
	0	10	20	30	40	50	60	70	80	90	100			
Market potential that can be realized							✓						30	
Required amount of promotional expense					✓								30	
Profit per unit			✓										20	
Contribution to sales of other products		✓											10	
Other contributions to firm's over-all program	✓												10	
Total													100	

FIGURE S–1. *Form for rating expectations of a new laboratory instrument.*

Case T: Converting Product Ratings to Volume Forecasts

Cordu-Velveteen Products Corporation

Cordu-Velveteen Products Corporation is engaged in the weaving and finishing of fashionable, high-quality corduroy and velveteen fabrics. For the coming selling season, sales are expected to total $100,000 per week. From a series of interviews, the following ratings have been obtained:

	Fabric A	Fabric B	Fabric C	Fabric D	Fabric E
Product Rating, Per Cent	40	20	80	50	30

Management does not question the sales forecast, as given above, but desires to ascertain:

1. The expected sales for each of the products, in dollars.
2. The expected "optimistic" or "high" sales volume, in dollars, representing a level 20 per cent above the "average expected" value given under 1 above.

PROBLEM

Perform the rating-to-volume conversion desired by management.

Index